# Collins

# AQA GCSE 9-1
# Design and Technology

## *Revision Guide*

Paul Anderson and David Hills-Taylor

# About this Revision & Practice book

## Revise

These pages provide a recap of everything you need to know for each topic.

You should read through all the information before taking the Quick Test at the end. This will test whether you can recall the key facts.

| Quick Test |
| --- |
| 1. What is iterative design? |
| 2. What are the advantages of user-centred design? |
| 3. When is the systems-based approach often used? |

## Practise

These topic-based questions appear shortly after the revision pages for each topic and will test whether you have understood the topic. If you get any of the questions wrong, make sure you read the correct answer carefully.

## Review

These topic-based questions appear later in the book, allowing you to revisit the topic and test how well you have remembered the information. If you get any of the questions wrong, make sure you read the correct answer carefully.

## Mix it Up

These pages feature a mix of exam-style questions for the different topics within a chapter. They will make sure you can recall the relevant information to answer a question without being told which topic it relates to.

## Test Yourself on the Go

Visit our website at **collins.co.uk/collinsGCSErevision** and print off a set of flashcards. These pocket-sized cards feature questions and answers so that you can test yourself on all the key facts anytime and anywhere. You will also find lots more information about the advantages of spaced practice and how to plan for it.

## Workbook

This section features even more topic-based questions as well as a practice exam paper, providing further practice opportunities for each topic to guarantee the best results.

## ebook

To access the ebook revision guide, visit

## collins.co.uk/ebooks

and follow the step-by-step instructions.

## QR Codes

Found throughout the book, the QR codes can be scanned on your smartphone for extra practice and explanations.

A QR code in the Revise section links to a Quick Recall Quiz on that topic. A QR code in the Workbook section links to a video working through the solution to one of the questions on that topic.

# Contents

# Contents

|  | Revise | | Practise | | Review | |
|---|---|---|---|---|---|---|

## Tools, Equipment and Processes

## New and Emerging Technologies

# Maths and Science Skills in the Exam

**You must be able to:**

- Use maths skills and science knowledge to answer questions related to Design & Technology.

Some of the exam questions for GCSE Design & Technology will use skills and knowledge that have been learned in maths and science. The following table summarises the maths skills and science knowledge that might be needed. It also gives some examples of how the maths skills might be used in questions in the exam. There are lots of practice questions that include maths skills in the relevant sections of this book. Look for the maths skills logo:

## Maths Skills

| Type of Maths | Skill or Knowledge | What This Might Be Used To Do |
|---|---|---|
| Arithmetic and Numerical Computation | 1a Recognise and use expressions in decimal and standard form | • Use decimal and standard form appropriately when using metric units and units of mass, length, time, money and other measures (for example $3.2 \times 10^3$ m). <br> • Calculate quantities and sizes of materials. <br> • Calculate costs of materials or energy sources. <br> • Select materials based on their mechanical properties or calculate properties needed. <br> • Calculate tolerances and seam allowances. |
| | 1b Use ratios, fractions and percentages | • Understand and use ratios in the scaling of drawings. <br> • Analyse provided tables and charts of data, such as survey responses and user questionnaires. <br> • Calculate percentages such as profit or waste savings. <br> • Calculate changes in the magnitude of forces when using mechanical devices. <br> • Calculate gear ratios. <br> • State the composition of important metal alloys. <br> • Use percentile ranges from anthropometric or ergonomic data to make design decisions. |
| | 1c Calculate surface areas and volumes (where dimensions are given) | • Determine quantities of materials needed, used or wasted. <br> • Calculate the volume of cuboids, and simple and composite shapes. |
| Handling Data | 2a Presentation of data, diagrams, bar charts and histograms | • Construct frequency tables using provided data. <br> • Interpret the meaning of data presented in frequency tables, for example to select materials or to determine user preferences from survey data. <br> • Present information on design decisions or client survey responses. <br> • Create tables of results and findings during prototype development. |

| Graphs | 3a Plot, draw and interpret graphs | • Analyse graphs to extract information and interpret what this information shows.<br>• Analyse responses to user questionnaires.<br>• Evaluate existing products using comparative charts of performance criteria.<br>• Plot or draw graphs from provided data (such as performance data or responses to client surveys). |
|---|---|---|
| | 3b Translate information between graph and number forms | • Extract information from provided technical specifications or graphs.<br>• Select materials.<br>• Identify tolerances for use in quality control. |
| Geometry and Trigonometry | 4a Using angular measurements in degrees | • Calculate angles and dimensions in components to support marking out.<br>• Calculate angles in structures reinforced by triangulation.<br>• Determine the angular movement of mechanisms.<br>• Create tessellated patterns that use material efficiently and minimise waste of material. |
| | 4b Visualise and represent 2D and 3D forms, including 2D representations of 3D objects | • Present design ideas.<br>• Communicate intentions to others.<br>• Represent the functions of mechanical devices producing different types of movement. |
| | 4c Calculate:<br>• areas of triangles<br>• areas of rectangles<br>• surface area and volumes of cubes | • Calculate the area or volume to determine quantities or sizes of materials needed. |

# Science Knowledge

Knowledge from science assists in presenting data appropriately and explaining the reasons for selecting and using materials (and energy sources).

| Science Topic | Knowledge |
|---|---|
| Use scientific vocabulary, terminology and definitions | 1a Quantities units and symbols |
| | 1b SI units |
| | 1c Differences between metals and non-metals based on their physical and chemical properties |
| Life cycle assessment and recycling | 2a Basic principles in carrying out a life cycle assessment |
| Using materials | 3a The conditions which cause corrosion and the process of corrosion and oxidation |
| | 3b The composition of some important alloys, their properties and uses |
| | 3c Physical properties of materials and how these are related to the use of materials |
| | 3d Main energy sources, how they are used and the difference between renewable and non-renewable sources |
| | 3e The action of forces and how levers and gears transmit and transform them |

# Design Strategies

**You must be able to:**

- Describe the main features of iterative design, user-centred design and a systems-based approach to design
- Explain the advantages and disadvantages of using each design strategy.

Approaches to Designing

## Different Design Strategies

- Design strategies are philosophies that guide how the design process takes place.
- Three of the most widely used design strategies are **iterative design**, **user-centred design** and **systems thinking**.
- Design strategies are important to avoid **design fixation**, which is when designers become overly attached to a particular idea.
- It is also important for specialists in different material areas to collaborate and share their expertise.
- Each different approach has its own advantages and disadvantages, which should be considered before they are put into practice.

## Iterative Design

- Iterative design is a cyclic approach.
- Each iteration of a design is tested and evaluated. Changes and refinements are then made, leading to a new iteration.
- Dyson vacuum cleaners are a good example of a product range designed using an iterative process. The original DC01 was developed as a result of thousands of different prototypes.

### Advantages of Iterative Design

- Because each iteration is fully tested and evaluated it is more likely that problems with the design will be discovered and dealt with earlier.
- It encourages focus on the most critical aspects of a product's design.
- User feedback is constantly being gathered.
- Evidence of progress in product design can be easily provided to stakeholders.

### Disadvantages of Iterative Design

- Designers can be so focused on the current iteration that they sometimes lose sight of the bigger design picture.
- It can be time consuming if a lot of prototypes or iterations need to be produced.

> **Key Point**
>
> Using an iterative design approach makes it more likely that problems with a design will be discovered earlier in the process.

Dyson make use of an iterative process when designing products

# User-Centred Design

- User-centred design is an approach where the needs and wants of the end user are considered extensively at each stage of the design process.

### Advantages of User-Centred Design

- The end user feels listened to and so has a greater sense of ownership of the final product.
- Listening to the end user at each design stage means it is more likely that the final product will meet users' expectations.

### Disadvantages of User-Centred Design

- It requires extra time to meet and hold discussions with users and then alter the design as a result of user feedback.
- If the design becomes too focused on a particular end user's requirements, it may become unviable to sell to the wider public.

# Systems Thinking

- The systems-based approach is often used when designing electronic, mechanical and mechatronic systems.
- It is a top-down approach that starts with an overview of the overall system in terms of its input, process and output sub-systems. The details of the individual components of each sub-system are considered later.

### Advantages of a Systems Approach

- It does not require highly specialist knowledge of electronic or mechanical components to design the overview of the system.
- The top-down approach makes it easy to communicate how the system will work to non-technical specialists, such as clients and stakeholders.
- The system is designed in blocks, so it is easier to find errors or faults in the design.

### Disadvantages of a Systems Approach

- Because of the block-based design approach, it can lead to the use of components that are not necessary.
- If unnecessary components are used it can lead to larger systems and extra cost.

Many electronic systems are designed using a systems-based approach

---

**Quick Test**

1. What is iterative design?
2. What are the advantages of user-centred design?
3. When is the systems-based approach often used?

# Electronic Systems

**You must be able to:**

- Describe the main stages that make up an electronic system
- Understand, select and use appropriate input, process and output devices in products.

## Structure of a System

- **Electronic systems** are usually made up of **input device**, **process** and **output device** stages. Some systems include a driver stage.
- Input devices take a 'real-world' signal, such as light, sound or movement, and turn it into an electronic signal, such as a voltage or current. Common examples are switches and sensors.
- Processes act like the 'brain' of a system. They alter the electronic signal to create functions such as timing and counting. Programmable components, such as **microcontrollers**, are commonly used as process devices in electronic systems.
- Drivers increase the signal going into the output stage of the system. This ensures that output devices can draw the required amount of current to work effectively.
- Output devices take an electronic signal and turn it into a real-world signal. For example, speakers produce sound and lamps produce light.

> **Key Point**
>
> Electronic systems consist of input, process and output stages, with drivers added as appropriate.

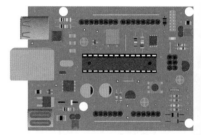

An electronic system assembled on a printed circuit board (PCB)

## Systems Block Diagrams

- Electronic systems can be represented as block diagrams.
- Block diagrams present a 'top-down' overview of the system and how it will work.
- The arrows represent the signals going into and out of each block.
- The blocks represent the components or groups of components that alter the signals.
- In the example, a light sensor, such as a light-dependent resistor (LDR), would detect the light level of the child's bedroom.

> **Key Point**
>
> Microcontrollers can be programmed to add functionality to products, such as timing and counting.

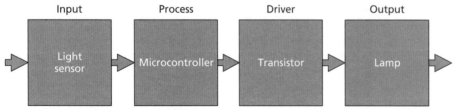

| Input | Process | Driver | Output |
|---|---|---|---|
| Light sensor | Microcontroller | Transistor | Lamp |

A block diagram for a child's night light

- The microcontroller could be programmed to turn the lamp on for a timed period when it gets dark. Microcontrollers can be programmed using flowchart software, block-based program editors or raw programming code.

A young child using a night light

# Electronic System Components

Some of the main components used in electronic systems are shown in the table.

| Component Name | Circuit Symbol | Input, Process or Output | What it Does |
|---|---|---|---|
| Push to make switch | | Input | Allows current to flow though it when pressed. |
| Light-dependent resistor | | Input | Has a resistance that changes depending on the light level. |
| Thermistor | | Input | Has a resistance that changes depending on the temperature. |
| Microcontroller | | Process | A small computer on an integrated circuit that can be programmed to provide functionality such as timing, counting and decision making. |
| Buzzer | | Output | Produces a buzzing sound when current flows through it. |
| Speaker | | Output | Turns electronic signals into sounds. |
| Lamp | | Output | Produces light when current flows through it. |

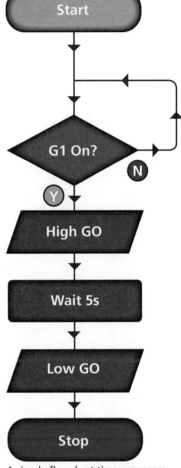

A simple flowchart timer program for a microcontroller. This program could be used to turn on a lamp for 5 seconds when a switch is pressed.

A light-dependent resistor (LDR)

## Quick Test

1. What are the four main stages that often make up a complete electronic system?
2. How do light-dependent resistors work?
3. What are the main methods of programming microcontrollers?
4. What output devices can be used to produce light and sound?

## Key Words

electronic system
input device
process
output device
microcontroller

# The Work of Others: Designers

**You must be able to:**

- Analyse and evaluate the work of at least two different designers
- Use the work of past and present designers to aid your own designing.

## Designers

| Name of Designer | About the Designer |
|---|---|
| Harry Beck | Designed the London Underground map in 1931. This was influenced by the layouts used in electronic schematics. The design has been widely copied for use in public transport systems across the world. |
| Marcel Breuer | An early student of the **Bauhaus** design school. Invented a new type of steel furniture inspired by bicycle handles. One famous example is the Wassily Chair. |
| Coco Chanel | A French fashion designer who founded the popular Chanel brand. The brand specialises in luxury items, fashion accessories and ready-to-wear clothing. The Chanel Suit is a famous example of their work. |
| Norman Foster | A British architect and founder of Foster + Partners. Designed the high-tech 'Gherkin' building in the City of London, which uses less than half of the energy of a similarly sized building. |
| Sir Alec Issigonis | A British-Greek car designer who designed the Mini, which is still hugely popular to this day. Also worked on the Morris Minor. |
| Alexander McQueen | A chief designer at Givenchy who also founded his own very successful design label. A fashion designer who was the British designer of the year four times. Many of his designs were controversial and used 'shock tactics'. |
| William Morris | A textile designer who was a leading player in the **Arts and Crafts** design movement. This movement was founded around the principles of traditional craftsmanship. |
| Mary Quant | An influential figure in the popular 60s Mod fashion movement. Encouraged people to dress to please themselves and treat fashion as a game. Took credit for the design of the miniskirt. |

A model wearing Chanel clothing at a fashion show

St Mary Axe, otherwise known as the 'Gherkin'

| Name of Designer | About the Designer |
|---|---|
| Charles Rennie Mackintosh | A Scottish architect and designer who was an influence on the **Art Nouveau** movement. He himself was influenced by modernist and Japanese architecture. An example of his work is 'The Lighthouse' building in Glasgow. |
| Gerrit Rietveld | A Dutch architect and furniture designer. He was influenced by and then joined the **De Stijl** design movement, which aimed to simplify design to vertical and horizontal lines, along with only using black, white and primary colours. Designed the famous Red and Blue Chair in 1917. |
| Aldo Rossi | Italian designer who achieved success in product design architecture, drawing and design theory. Author of the seminal urban design book, *The Architecture of the City*, published in 1966. |
| Ettore Sottsass | Founder of the Italian Memphis design group in 1981. **Memphis** designs incorporated asymmetric shapes and colourful decoration. The 1969 'Typewriter Valentine' is a well-known early example of his work. |
| Philippe Starck | A French designer who is known for his interior product and furniture designs. Designed the 'Juicy Salif' lemon squeezer in 1990 for Alessi, which is now widely seen as a design icon. |
| Raymond Templier | A French jewellery designer inspired by the Art Deco movement. He typically paired dark stones and precious white metals to create bold geometric pieces. |
| Louis Comfort Tiffany | American designer and metalworker associated with the Art Nouveau movement. Worked as design director at Tiffany and Co. who are well known for their successful jewellery and lamp designs. |
| Vivienne Westwood | A British fashion designer who was influential in the punk fashion styles of the 1970s. Was later a major player in the New Romantic and New Wave pop culture fashions that followed, widely credited with bringing them into the mainstream. |

A spiral staircase inside 'The Lighthouse', a building in Glasgow designed by Charles Rennie Mackintosh

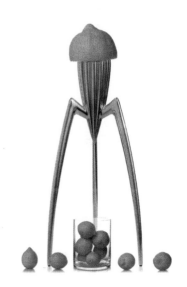

Philippe Starck's 'Juicy Salif' lemon squeezer

## Key Point

Understanding the work of past and present designers helps new designers to inform their own work.

## Key Words

**Bauhaus**
**Arts and Crafts**
**Art Nouveau**
**De Stijl**
**Memphis**

## Quick Test

1. Who designed 30 St Mary Axe, known as the 'Gherkin'?
2. What design school was Marcel Breuer a student of?
3. Who wrote the design book *The Architecture of the City*?
4. Who designed the Mini car?

# The Work of Others: Companies

Quick Recall Quiz

**You must be able to:**

- Analyse and evaluate the work of at least two different design companies
- Use the work of design companies to aid your own designing.

## Companies

| Name of Company | About the Company |
|---|---|
| Alessi | <ul><li>An Italian design company that produces everyday houseware and kitchen utensils designed by famous names.</li><li>Many of its products are in the 'post-modern' style.</li><li>A famous example of one of its products is the 'Juicy Salif' lemon squeezer designed by Philippe Starck.</li></ul> |
| Apple | <ul><li>A multinational consumer electronics company based in California, USA. Founded by Steve Jobs, Steve Wozniak and Ronald Wayne in 1976.</li><li>Initially the company sold personal computers, such as the Macintosh. This was extremely innovative at the time due to the use of a graphical user interface and mouse.</li><li>Later Apple produced the **aesthetically** iconic iMac G3, the iPod portable digital music player and the hugely successful iPhone, which combined elements of both the G3 and the iPod with a touch-screen mobile phone.</li></ul> |
| Braun | <ul><li>A German company that produces a range of consumer products.</li><li>Founded by Max Braun, a mechanical engineer in 1921, initially to produce radios.</li><li>Well known today for its shaving and grooming products and for functional approach to design.</li></ul> |
| Dyson | <ul><li>A British design engineering company.</li><li>Formed by James Dyson in 1991 as a way of bringing his new bagless vacuum cleaner invention to the market. By 2001 over 47% of all vacuum cleaners sold in the UK were Dysons.</li><li>As well as being bagless, Dyson vacuum cleaners do not lose suction due to their unique cyclone dust-separation technology.</li><li>Dyson has since diversified its product line to include heaters, bladeless fans and even hairdryers.</li></ul> |

The iMac G3 became aesthetically iconic due to its bold colours and curved shape

A Dyson cordless vacuum cleaner

### Key Point

Understanding the work of design companies helps new designers to inform their own work.

| Name of Company | About the Company |
|---|---|
| Gap | • Gap, styled as GAP, is an American clothing and accessories company that trades throughout the world.<br>• Although it initially targeted a younger audience, it now serves a broader age range of people.<br>• Much of its sales come from its website, which attracts over 18 million visitors a year. |
| Primark | • An international clothing retailer with its main base located in Dublin, Ireland.<br>• Known for its low-cost yet fashionable products, and its contribution to the modern **'fast fashion'** trend.<br>• Primark's clothes are made in places such as China, India and Bangladesh. It does not own the factories that produce its clothing. |
| Under Armour | • An American sportswear company formed in 1996 by Kevin Plank, former American football player.<br>• Developed **moisture-wicking** sportswear that uses microfibres to keep athletes cool and dry.<br>• Now also sells footwear, casual clothing and accessories. |
| Zara | • A Spanish clothing and accessories company founded by Amancio Ortega and Rosalía Mera.<br>• Known for selling products that react to current consumer trends, using a 'just-in-time' production approach.<br>• Began working with Greenpeace in 2011 to eliminate harmful toxins from its clothing. |

The Primark logo

An Under Armour shop front

## Quick Test

1. What was special about the first Apple iPhone?
2. What did James Dyson initially invent?
3. What is Under Armour sportswear designed to do?
4. What did Zara begin working on with Greenpeace in 2011?

## Key Words

aesthetics
'fast fashion'
moisture-wicking fabric

# Ecological, Environmental and Social Issues

**You must be able to:**

- Explain how designing and making is affected by ecological, environmental and social issues
- Discuss the benefits of fair trade for producers and consumers.

## Ecological Issues in the Design and Manufacture of Products

- Designers must consider how the raw materials used in products are sourced and the wider ecological effects of each of these processes.
  - **Deforestation** is when forests are removed and the land is converted to other uses. This results in the loss of habitats for animals and other species. It can also impact on climate change.
  - Some raw materials must be mined from the ground. An example of this is metal ore. Mining can cause erosion and the contamination of soil. The appearance of some sinkholes can be traced back to mining activities.
  - Oil is needed to make plastics and must be drilled for. The biggest potential problem with this process is when oil spills occur. These can have devastating effects on the local environment and on people's health.
  - Some raw materials, such as those used in biofuels, are farmed. Over-farming and use of pesticides can lead to the contamination of land and the death of wildlife.
- Carbon is released into the atmosphere from producing products. This is widely accepted as a cause of global warming.
- Designers must also consider the distance, or mileage, that a product travels, from the source of its raw materials to the place of manufacture, distribution, use and final disposal.

A sea-based oil drilling platform

### Key Point

The 6 Rs can be used to help designers evaluate the impact of their products on the environment.

## The 6 Rs

- The 6 Rs of sustainability is a tool widely used to help designers reduce the impact of their products on the environment. It can be used as a checklist for each product that is designed.
  - **Reduce** – How can the amount of materials and components used in the product be reduced? Is the product itself necessary?
  - **Rethink** – How can the design of the product be changed so that it is less harmful to the environment? Can a better way to solve the problem be found?
  - **Refuse** – Should the product be produced if it is not sustainably designed? Is the packaging necessary or can it be removed?
  - **Recycle** – Is the product made using recycled materials? Could the materials be recycled once the product is no longer useful?

The Mobius loop symbol shows that a product can be recycled

- **Reuse** – Could the product be used in a different way once its current use has expired? Could it be disassembled so that its materials and components could be reused in other products?
- **Repair** – Is the product easy to repair? Are replacement components readily available in case of failure?

# Social Issues in the Design and Manufacture of Products

- The design and manufacture of products can also have effects on wider society. Designers should consider the social footprint of the products that they produce.
- It is important that workers who manufacture products are kept safe while doing so. In the UK there is strict legislation designed to ensure that employers look after the safety of their workers. However, workers in some countries where products are produced are not subject to the same protections.
- **Atmospheric pollution** occurs when pollutants are released into the Earth's atmosphere. Air pollution has been linked to severe respiratory illnesses in people, such as lung cancer and asthma.
- **Oceanic pollution** happens when chemicals and other industrial waste is released into the oceans. This has a negative impact on marine life and habitats.
- Designers and manufacturers should consider ways to reduce the amount of pollution that their products cause at each stage of their life. Some people may choose not to buy a product if they think it has not been designed or made in a socially considerate manner.

Air pollution can have negative effects on people's health

## Key Point

Fair trade helps people in developing countries to get a fair deal for the products that they produce.

# Fair Trade

- **Fair trade** is a movement that works to help people in developing countries get a fair deal for the products that they produce.
- Producers are paid an agreed minimum rate for many products. This gets paid even if global prices fall.
- They also receive a Fairtrade Premium payment that they can use to invest in areas such as local education and healthcare.
- Many consumers like to buy fair trade products as it fits with their values and principles.
- The Fairtrade Certification Mark shows that a product meets fair trade standards.

The Fairtrade Certification Mark placed on imported bananas

## Quick Test

1. What are the 6 Rs of sustainability?
2. What are the main benefits of fair trade for producers of products?
3. What are the potential impacts of oceanic pollution?

## Key Words

deforestation
recycle
atmospheric pollution
oceanic pollution
fair trade

# Practice Questions

## Design Strategies and Electronic Systems

**1**    **1.1)**   Complete the table below by entering a suitable electronic component to achieve each function.

State whether each is an input, process or output.

| Function | Component | Input, Process or Output |
|---|---|---|
| Detect changes in light level | | |
| Produce light | | |
| Produce sound | | |
| Detect changes in temperature | | |
| Be programmed to turn an output on for a set period of time | | |

[10]

**1.2)**   Define what is meant by 'user-centred design'.

_____

_____

_____

[1]

# The Work of Others: Designers

**2** Give the names of **two** past or present designers. For each, give the name of a design that they have created and explain the influence of this design.

Designer 1 .............................................................................................................................................

..................................................................................................................................................................

Design .....................................................................................................................................................

..................................................................................................................................................................

..................................................................................................................................................................

..................................................................................................................................................................

Influence ................................................................................................................................................

..................................................................................................................................................................

..................................................................................................................................................................

.................................................................................................................................................... **[4]**


Designer 2 .............................................................................................................................................

..................................................................................................................................................................

Design .....................................................................................................................................................

..................................................................................................................................................................

..................................................................................................................................................................

..................................................................................................................................................................

Influence ................................................................................................................................................

..................................................................................................................................................................

..................................................................................................................................................................

.................................................................................................................................................... **[4]**

## The Work of Others: Companies

**3** Give the names of **two** design companies. For each, give the name of a design that they have created and explain the influence of this design.

Company 1 ..........................................................................................................................

..............................................................................................................................................

Design ...............................................................................................................................

..............................................................................................................................................

..............................................................................................................................................

Influence ...........................................................................................................................

..............................................................................................................................................

..............................................................................................................................................

..............................................................................................................................................
[4]


Company 2 ..........................................................................................................................

..............................................................................................................................................

Design ...............................................................................................................................

..............................................................................................................................................

..............................................................................................................................................

Influence ...........................................................................................................................

..............................................................................................................................................

..............................................................................................................................................

..............................................................................................................................................
[4]

# Ecological, Environmental and Social Issues

**4** The 6 Rs are used to help designers improve the sustainability of the products that they produce.

Define the meaning of each of the 6 Rs.

Reuse

Recycle

Refuse

Rethink

Reduce

Repair

[6]

Total Marks _____ / 33

# Research and Investigation

**You must be able to:**

- Describe the main methods of conducting research and investigation
- Explain the difference between primary and secondary data
- Describe the use of ergonomics and anthropometric data when researching and designing products.

## Conducting Research and Investigation

- Designers carry out research and investigation to find out more about the design problem and the needs of the market, client and/or end user.
- Ways of doing this include market research, client interviews, focus groups and product analysis.
  - **Market research** is when information is collected to find out whether there is a place in the market for a proposed product. A product that is first to market can quickly become very successful. An example of this is the first mobile phone made by Motorola in 1973. This propelled them from being a small company into the position of market leaders for over two decades.
  - It is important to discuss the client's requirements directly with them. Interviews can be face-to-face or via virtual meeting technology if travelling long distances is an issue.
  - A focus group is a group of people assembled to discuss and give feedback on a product or a design idea. These people are often potential consumers of the product.
  - Designers can learn a lot from the successes and failures of current or previous products. Product analysis is the detailed investigation or analysis of these designs. As well as looking at how products look and function, this should also include their wider impact on society and the environment.

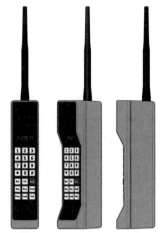

Motorola produced the first working mobile phone in 1973, resulting in them becoming market leaders for over two decades

### Key Point

Designers must check to see if there is a gap in the market for their products.

## Gathering Data

- When completing research and investigation designers use different types of data.
- **Primary data** is raw data taken first hand or from original research. For example, a designer could ask a group of people to answer a questionnaire about a proposed solution to a design problem. Responses to this could then be analysed and the findings discussed.
- **Secondary data** is data that is freely available and taken from other parties or sources. For example, datasheets and catalogues can provide useful information about the technical aspects of the raw materials to be used.

# Ergonomics and Anthropometrics

### Ergonomics

- **Ergonomics**, otherwise known as human factors, is about understanding how people interact with the products and systems around them. It is a key factor in ensuring that a product is easy to use.
- When considering ergonomics, designers will think about factors such as comfort and safety. For example, the handle of a garden tool can be designed so that it fits comfortably in the hand.

### Anthropometric Data

- **Anthropometrics** is the study of the human body and how it moves.
- Anthropometric data is measurements taken from millions of people of different shapes and sizes and placed in charts.
- Measurements include hip height, shoulder height, head circumference and hand length.
- Designers can make use of these charts when designing products and systems. For example, when designing head gear making use of head circumference sizes can ensure the product fits the people it is intended for.
- When using anthropometric data, designers will often work from the 5th to the 95th percentile. This ensures that 90% of the population are catered for.

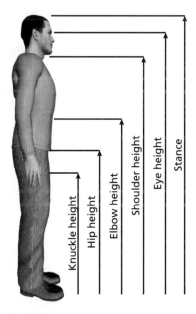

Anthropometric data

 **Key Point**

Designers use anthropometric data to ensure that product dimensions are correct for the people who will use them.

 **Key Words**

market research
primary data
secondary data
ergonomics
anthropometric data

### Quick Test

1. What is a focus group?
2. What is the difference between primary and secondary data?
3. What is anthropometric data and how is it used in the design of products and systems?

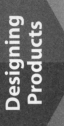
# Briefs and Specifications

**You must be able to:**

- Write a design brief and design specification for a product or system
- Modify a design brief as a result of user feedback
- Produce a manufacturing specification for a product or system.

## Design Brief and Design Specification

- Once the design context has been thoroughly explored, a **design brief** and **design specification** should be written.
- When doing this, designers should consider the needs, wants and interests of the **end users** of the product or system.

> ### Key Point
>
> A design brief gives a short description of the problem that is to be solved.

## Design Brief

- The design brief is a short description of the design problem and how it is to be solved.
- The design situation is usually outlined first, followed by the brief itself.
- It is typically written as a few sentences or a short paragraph. For example:

| Situation |
|---|
| Developing numeracy skills early in life equips young children well for when they start school. Many of these skills can be learned through play. |

| Brief |
|---|
| I am going to design and make a toy for young children aged 3–5 years. The toy must be interactive and educational to the child. It should help them to improve their numeracy skills. |

A toy designed to help build the numeracy skills of young children

### Modifying a Design Brief

- Sometimes when investigating the needs of users, it becomes apparent that the design brief is not appropriate and should be altered. This could be as a result of specific end user feedback.
- It is important to meet with the end user to speak about their requirements. These responses can then be discussed with other designers on the team. A spider chart is good way to record these thoughts.
- It is much better to make changes at an early stage. Failing to do this could result in a lot of time, money and materials being wasted on a product that is ultimately not fit for purpose.

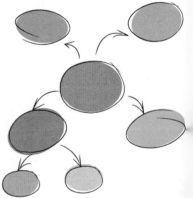

A spider chart

# Design Specification

- A design specification is a list of measurable design criteria that the product or system must meet. It is usually written as a set of bullet points.
- It provides much more detail on the specific requirements of the product or system.
- A good specification will include criteria related to cost, aesthetics, function, ergonomics, quality and the materials and components to be used. It may also consider social, environmental and sustainability requirements.
- ACCESS FM is a useful tool for writing a design specification:
  - **Aesthetics** – How will the product appeal to the five senses?
  - **Client** – Who is the product for? What gender and age range do they fall into?
  - **Cost** – How much will it cost to manufacture the product? What will be the cost to the consumer?
  - **Environment** – How will the product impact on the environment? How can it be designed and made so that it is more sustainable?
  - **Safety** – How will the product be designed so that it is safe to use?
  - **Size** – What will be the dimensions in millimetres of the finished product?
  - **Function** – What will the product do and how will it work?
  - **Materials** – What materials and components will be used to manufacture the product?

> **Key Point**
>
> ACCESS FM is a tool that can be used to help designers to write a design specification.

# Manufacturing Specification

- The manufacturing specification should contain the information needed to successfully manufacture the design. It should include the following:
  - The scale of production to be used: is the product to be batch or mass produced, or made as a one-off item?
  - A description and/or drawing of the final design. This should include assembly and construction details.
  - Details of the materials and components that are needed: will any standard components be used?
  - Details of how quality will be ensured, such as quality control and quality assurance.

A manufacturing specification gives the details needed to make a product

> **Key Words**
>
> design brief
> design specification
> end user
> manufacturing specification

# Exploring and Developing Ideas

**You must be able to:**

- Describe the main stages of developing a design idea
- Explain the use of card models, toiles and breadboards.

## Using an Iterative Process

- An iterative process is often used when exploring and developing design ideas. More information on an iterative design approach can be found on page 8 of this revision guide.
- Designers produce sketches and models of their ideas as part of this process.
- Testing and evaluation allows refinements and improvements to be made to designs.

## Sketching

- Freehand sketching is a good way to get initial thoughts and ideas down on paper.
- As sketches don't have to follow conventions they can be drawn quickly. They can be annotated and labelled to convey important information about the design.
- Once sketches of initial ideas have been completed, a more formal presentation drawing can be completed.

Sketching an idea

## Modelling

- A model is a representation of a product or system that is being developed.
- Designers make **models** of their ideas to check how they will look and function in 3D. They can also be presented to clients and stakeholders to gain feedback.
- Making models ensures that problems with the design are found early, before the design is manufactured using more expensive materials.

> ### Key Point
>
> Modelling is a key part of the iterative design process.

### Card Models

- Card is commonly used for making early or rough models of a design as it is cheap and easy to cut.
- Card can be cut using scissors or craft knives. Safety rulers and/ or rotary trimmers can be used when straight lines are needed.
- Pieces of card can be attached together using masking tape or hot glue guns.

Card can be cut accurately using a craft knife

## Toiles

- **Toiles** are widely used in the textiles and fashion industry.
- A toile is a test version of a piece of clothing made from cheap materials.
- They are made to check the effectiveness of a pattern that has been produced for a garment.
- This can then be evaluated and the pattern improved without wasting more expensive materials.

## Breadboarding Circuits

- Electronic circuits can be modelled by **breadboarding**.
- Breadboards consist of rows of conducting metal strips, covered by plastic with holes. Components and wires are placed into these holes to create a circuit.

A circuit prototype produced using breadboard

- No soldering is involved, so circuits can be quickly tested, changed or updated as required. Components can be reused as many times as needed.
- The advantage of breadboarding over modelling using computer-aided design (CAD; see pages 32–33 and 124–125 of this revision guide) is that it uses real components. Not all CAD simulation software is 100% accurate. Often designers will produce both CAD models and physical prototypes of a circuit for this reason.
- It is a temporary circuit construction method, so should not be used for a final circuit that is to be placed in a product. A more permanent construction method, such as producing a printed circuit board (PCB), should be used for this purpose.

 **Key Point**

Breadboarding is a method of prototyping electronic circuits.

# Testing and Evaluation

- Each iteration of a design should be tested and evaluated to assess how well it does the job that it is supposed to do.
- The client or end user should be involved in this process as their feedback is very important.
- Once testing and evaluation has been completed, refinements should be made to the design. This results in the next iteration of the design being developed.

## Quick Test

1. What are the main stages of developing a design?
2. Why do designers produce sketches of their ideas?
3. Why are toiles made?
4. What is the main advantage of breadboarding over CAD circuit modelling?

 **Key Words**

model
toile
breadboarding

# Communication of Ideas 1

**You must be able to:**

- Produce sketches using perspective and isometric projection
- Describe how to produce an exploded drawing
- Annotate a drawing effectively to explain features of a design.

## Sketching

- Freehand sketching is a quick method of creating and communicating design ideas.
- Freehand sketches do not have to follow conventions; for example, they don't need to be to scale or include exact details.

## 3D Sketching

- 3D sketches can be produced freehand, by using **perspective** or by **isometric projection**.
- Perspective drawing can be used to produce a realistic view of a product, for example to show to a client.
- The drawing is not to scale.
- It has a horizon line, also known as an eyeline.
- One or two vanishing points sit on the horizon line (for one- or two-point perspective).
- Non-vertical lines in the object can be extended to meet at the vanishing point.
- One-point perspective is often used for interiors.
- Isometric projection can be used to produce a 3D object to scale. It uses lines at 30° to the baseline (60° to the edges). Isometric paper has a grid which can be used as guidelines.

Horizon line / eye line

Vanishing point

> **Key Point**
>
> Sketches are a quick method to create and communicate design ideas.

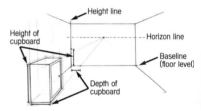

One-point perspective drawing

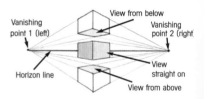

Two-point perspective drawing

## Exploded Drawings

- **Exploded drawings** (also known as exploded views) show how the parts of a product fit together.
- The parts should be lined up and the correct size relative to the other parts.

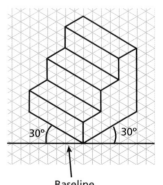

Isometric drawing

- They are especially useful to people who are assembling products made from lots of different parts. They are often included, for example, in the instructions for furniture that the user has to put together themselves.

## Annotation

- **Annotation** means adding notes and labels to drawings and sketches.
- These should not just be descriptive; for example, colours or materials. They should explain the detailed development of the design, such as the design decisions made.
- Examples of sentence starters for good annotation include:
  - *This meets/doesn't meet my design specification requirements because …*
  - *The colours and finishes I would use are … and would be applied by …*
  - *This would cost less if …*
  - *To make sure this is safe I would have to …*
  - *This could be made from … because …*
  - *The processes used to make this feature would be … because …*
  - *This is easy/difficult to make because …*
  - *This design was inspired by …*
  - *I like/don't like this design because …*

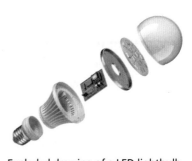

Exploded drawing of a LED lightbulb

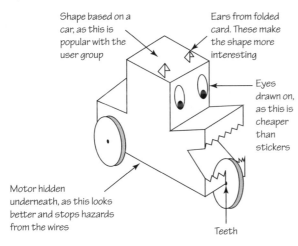

My ideas all used an animal theme. This idea is a dog.

Shape based on a car, as this is popular with the user group

Ears from folded card. These make the shape more interesting

Eyes drawn on, as this is cheaper than stickers

Motor hidden underneath, as this looks better and stops hazards from the wires

Teeth

Annotated sketches for a novelty toy vehicle

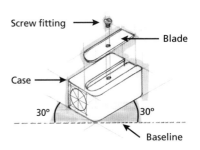

Screw fitting

Blade

Case

30°    30°

Baseline

Exploded isometric drawing of a pencil sharpener

**Quick Test**

1. Name three methods used to produce 3D sketches.
2. What angle to the baseline are the lines on an isometric projection?
3. What is the purpose of an exploded drawing?

# Communication of Ideas 2

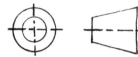

## You must be able to:

- Use and produce working drawings
- Describe how mathematical modelling and computer-based tools are used to communicate design ideas
- Explain how ideas can be physically modelled.

## Working Drawings

- **Working drawings**, also known as orthographic drawings, are used to communicate the sizes of the item drawn.
- There are conventions that state how they should be drawn. These help to avoid misunderstandings. They are set out in British Standard BS8888:2006.
- Third-angle **orthographic projection** shows three views of an object – plan (top), front and side – arranged as shown in the illustration of the house.
- The drawing should be to scale and include all the dimensions needed to make the product.
- Scale is written as a ratio. An object drawn half the size of the original is 1:2. An object drawn twice the size of the original is 2:1.

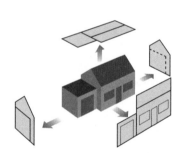

Third-angle orthographic projection

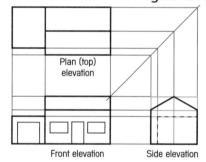

Front elevation   Side elevation

Plan (top) elevation

Symbol for third-angle projection

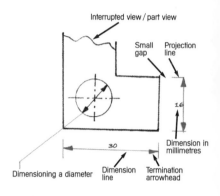

Dimensions on working drawings

## System and Schematic Drawings

- Systems diagrams can be used to show the concept of how a system will work. It should include the input, process and output blocks and the signal that passes through them. A systems diagram may also include a feedback loop.
- Schematic diagrams represent the elements of a system using standard symbols rather than pictures. They show which components are linked together and are commonly used to represent electrical circuits or pneumatic systems.

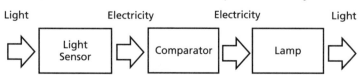

Systems diagram

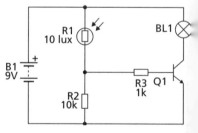

Schematic drawing of the circuit represented in the systems diagram

# Mathematical Modelling

- A **mathematical model** is a way of simulating real-life situations using maths formulae.
- Mathematical models can be used to demonstrate how a product or system works, how a system will change if it is modified or how a product should be designed for optimum performance.
- Uses range from calculating the values of components to use in an electrical circuit to designing the shape of speedboat hulls, determining how strong a bridge needs to be and simulating the testing of aircraft in wind tunnels.

## Computer-Based Tools

- Orthographic drawings are typically produced using computer-aided design, or CAD, software.
- Virtual models, also produced using 3D CAD software, can be used to test how well parts fit together.
- Most mathematical models and simulations are carried out by computers, as they involve quite complicated formulae and many calculations.

## Physical Modelling

- Physical modelling involves making a prototype of the design idea.
- Card models can be used to quickly and cheaply give an impression of the physical size and shape of a product.
- When designing textile garments, a toile is often made from low-cost fabric (such as calico). This tests the pattern and fit without using the more expensive fabric that the garment will be made from.
- Breadboarding is used to construct electronic circuits, as parts can be quickly swapped or moved to test different ideas.

## Other Ways of Communicating Ideas

- Film clips or audio recordings can be used to communicate design features and concepts. These might include interviews with the clients or users, explaining their needs or giving feedback.

> **Key Point**
>
> Systems diagrams represent the system blocks that change the signal. Schematic diagrams show all the elements within the system blocks.

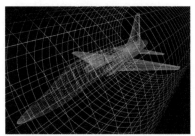
Simulated testing of how an aircraft will perform in a wind tunnel

### Quick Test

1. Name the three views shown on a third-angle orthographic projection.
2. Give two examples of how mathematical models are used.
3. Name three methods used to make a physical model of a design idea.

> **Key Words**
>
> working drawing
> orthographic projection
> mathematical model

# Computer-Based Tools

**You must be able to:**

- Explain the effects and benefits of computer-based tools when communicating ideas
- Describe how computer-based tools can be used to share and present ideas and technical information.

## Effects of Computer-Based Tools on Communication

- Computer-based and digital tools have revolutionised how designers communicate with clients, end users and each other.
- From sharing designs to holding virtual meetings with people on the other side of the world, digital technology has enabled designers to share and discuss ideas with almost anyone, almost anywhere in the world.

## Meeting with Clients and Other Stakeholders

- Designers regularly communicate with clients and other stakeholders during the designing and making process. They also communicate with other designers who have different specialisms or expertise that they can learn from.
- In the past, distance could be a problem when doing this. Travelling to other parts of the world can be very expensive and time consuming.
- Designers can email questions to clients but there may be a long wait for a response, particularly when communicating across different time zones. In addition, sometimes raw text can be misinterpreted.
- **Virtual meeting software** allows face-to-face meetings to take place from different locations. This can be via wired, wireless or mobile networks. Some mobile apps are designed for this specific purpose.

## Presenting Ideas to Clients

- A key part of the design process is gaining end-user or client feedback. This is particularly important when using design strategies such as user-centred design.
- Face-to-face presentations are still a very important part of this process.

> ### Key Point
>
> Virtual meeting technologies allow designers to meet with clients almost anywhere in the world.

A virtual meeting by mobile phone

A designer presenting potential solutions to clients

- **Presentation software** can be used to create visual aids for a presentation. These add interest for viewers and allow the sharing of photographs, images and technical information related to a design solution.
- Image-manipulation software can be used to prepare photographs of a design or prototype for a presentation.

# Use of CAD/CAM

- Computer-aided design (CAD) software can be used to draw, model and simulate design ideas.
- Simulations are particularly useful when communicating with clients, as they show how the product or system will work. For example, a designer could demonstrate how both the electronic components and outer casing would function in a new idea for a task light.
- CAD software also allows design ideas to be viewed from different angles.
- CAD files can be sent directly to computer-aided manufacture (CAM; see pages 124–125 of this revision guide) and rapid prototyping machines to create a quick 3D representation of a design. This can then be shared with potential clients.
- CAD files can be shared using email, intranets, USB memory sticks or via the cloud. It important that these are password-protected to ensure the idea does not fall into the wrong hands.

Designers using rapid prototyping equipment

# Use of Spreadsheet Software

- **Spreadsheet software** simplifies the creation of data tables and calculations. This saves time and money for designers.
- One example of the use of spreadsheet software is the creation of a bill of materials for a product or system. The materials and components can be listed along with their purchasing costs. The total cost can then be calculated automatically.
- Graphs can be created easily from the data, such as a line graph to demonstrate potential profits per year to stakeholders.

Spreadsheet software being used to calculate costs

**Key Point**

Spreadsheet software can be used to share data relating to a design solution.

**Quick Test**

1. What are the benefits of virtual meeting software?
2. How does presentation software help designers communicate?
3. Give an example of the use of spreadsheet software in design and technology.

**Key Words**

**virtual meeting software**
**presentation software**
**spreadsheet software**

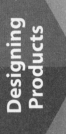
# Prototype Development

Quick Recall Quiz

**You must be able to:**

- Explain why designers produce prototypes
- Explain the considerations that need to be taken account of when developing prototypes
- Describe and explain how a prototype of a product or system can be evaluated.

## Prototypes

- **Prototypes** are full-sized, actual versions or primary examples of an intended product or system.
- They differ from models, which are usually scaled down representations of a product.
- Designers make prototypes to check how a product or system will look and function. They can also be presented to clients to gain their feedback.
- Making prototypes ensures that problems with a design are found early, before too much time and money are spent on materials and manufacture.
- There are several considerations that designers must take account of when developing a prototype:
  - Does it satisfy the requirements of the brief, the specification and the client? Has the client been consulted or given feedback on the prototype?
  - Is the prototype innovative or creative? Will it offer something original to the market?
  - Does it function as expected? Is it fit for its intended purpose?
  - Is it aesthetically pleasing? How does it appeal to the five senses?
  - Is it easily marketable? Will it fill a gap in the market?

## Evaluating Prototypes

- **Evaluation** helps the designer to learn about how well the product being prototyped would meet the needs of the specification and the client.
- It is important for designers to react critically when evaluating prototypes and responding to feedback.
- Evaluation and improvement is an ongoing process from inception all the way to final product manufacture.
- Evaluation should result in improvements or refinements being made to the design.

> ### Key Point
>
> Making prototypes ensures that problems with a design are found and dealt with early on.

Dyson are well known for their use of prototyping when designing and producing new products, such as the bladeless fan

## CAFÉ QUE

- CAFÉ QUE is a useful tool for evaluating a prototype of a product or system.
    - **Cost** – What is the cost of the materials and components used in the prototype? Will the final product be good value for money for the client or consumer?
    - **Aesthetics** – How well does the prototype appeal to the five senses? How visually appealing is it to the target market?
    - **Function** – How well does the prototype work? How well does it do its intended job? How has this been tested?
    - **Ergonomics** – How well have usability and human factors been considered?
    - **Quality** – Is the prototype of a suitable or required quality? How will quality be ensured when manufacturing the final product?
    - **User** – Who is the intended user of the final product? Does the prototype in its current form meet their needs? If not, how must it be modified?
    - **Environment** – How sustainable is the prototype? Is it made from recycled materials? Could the materials and components be easily reused? Does it use biodegradable materials?

It is important to speak with the end user or client about how well the prototype meets their needs

**Quick Test**

1. What is a prototype?
2. Why is client feedback of a prototype important?
3. Why are prototypes evaluated?

**Key Words**

prototype
evaluation

# Review Questions

## Design Strategies, and Ecological, Environmental and Social Issues

**1**   **1.1)**   Explain **one** benefit of fair trade to producers of products.

.......................................................................................................................................

.......................................................................................................................................

.......................................................................................................................................

.......................................................................................................................................   [2]

**1.2)**   Explain why a consumer might choose **not** to buy a fair trade product.

.......................................................................................................................................

.......................................................................................................................................

.......................................................................................................................................

.......................................................................................................................................   [2]

**1.3)**   Define the term 'deforestation'.

.......................................................................................................................................

.......................................................................................................................................   [1]

**1.4)**   Explain what is meant by iterative design.

.......................................................................................................................................

.......................................................................................................................................

.......................................................................................................................................

.......................................................................................................................................   [2]

# Electronic Systems

**2** A design is being produced for a doorbell system. A programmable component is to be used to control how the system works. The programmable system must:

- Detect when a switch has been pressed.

- Activate a buzzer for a period of 5 seconds after the switch has been pressed.

- Turn off the buzzer after the time period has ended.

- Turn on a lamp after the buzzer has stopped sounding.

Write a program that meets the needs of the doorbell system described above. You may use any programming language that you are familiar with.

[6]

# Review Questions

## The Work of Others: Designers

**3** Identify **two** past or present designers. For each describe the impact that they have had on the design world.

Designer 1 .......................................................................................................................................

.............................................................................................................................................................

Impact .............................................................................................................................................

.............................................................................................................................................................

.............................................................................................................................................................

.............................................................................................................................................................

.............................................................................................................................................................

.............................................................................................................................................  [4]

Designer 2 .......................................................................................................................................

.............................................................................................................................................................

Impact .............................................................................................................................................

.............................................................................................................................................................

.............................................................................................................................................................

.............................................................................................................................................................

.............................................................................................................................................................

.............................................................................................................................................  [4]

# The Work of Others: Companies

**4** Identify **two** design companies. For each, name and describe a product that they have designed.

Company 1 .............................................................................................................................

.................................................................................................................................................

Product .................................................................................................................................

.................................................................................................................................................

Description ...........................................................................................................................

.................................................................................................................................................

.................................................................................................................................................

.................................................................................................................................................

.................................................................................................................................... **[4]**

Company 2 .............................................................................................................................

.................................................................................................................................................

Product .................................................................................................................................

.................................................................................................................................................

Description ...........................................................................................................................

.................................................................................................................................................

.................................................................................................................................................

.................................................................................................................................... **[4]**

Total Marks ................... / 29

# Practice Questions

## Research and Investigation

**1** **1.1)** What is anthropometric data?

........................................................................................................................................

........................................................................................................................................

........................................................................................................................................ [2]

**1.2)** A designer is creating an idea for a new helmet for firefighters. Explain how anthropometric data could be used to help the designer.

........................................................................................................................................

........................................................................................................................................

........................................................................................................................................

........................................................................................................................................ [3]

**1.3)** State the meaning of each of the following:

Primary data

........................................................................................................................................

........................................................................................................................................

Secondary data

........................................................................................................................................

........................................................................................................................................ [3]

# Briefs and Specifications

**2**  **2.1)**  Which of the following sentences best describes a design brief?
Tick the correct box.

    **a.** Data placed in tables that can be used in the design of the product. ☐

    **b.** A set of information about how the product is to be manufactured. ☐

    **c.** A set of measurable design targets that the product must meet. ☐

    **d.** A short description of the design problem and how it is to be solved. ☐ [1]

**2.2)**  Which of the following sentences best describes a design specification?
Tick the correct box.

    **a.** Data placed in tables that can be used in the design of the product. ☐

    **b.** A set of information about how the product is to be manufactured. ☐

    **c.** A set of measurable design targets that the product must meet. ☐

    **d.** A short description of the design problem and how it is to be solved. ☐ [1]

**2.3)**  Which of the following sentences best describes a manufacturing specification?
Tick the correct box.

    **a.** Data placed in tables that can be used in the design of the product. ☐

    **b.** A set of information about how the product is to be manufactured. ☐

    **c.** A set of measurable design targets that the product must meet. ☐

    **d.** A short description of the design problem and how it is to be solved. ☐ [1]

## Exploring and Developing Ideas

**3** **3.1)** Name an appropriate method of modelling each of the following.

An electronic circuit

.................................................................................................................................................... [1]

A wedding dress

.................................................................................................................................................... [1]

An early idea for a mobile phone case

.................................................................................................................................................... [1]

**3.2)** Other than modelling, name **three** other stages of developing a design idea.

**1.** ................................................................................................................................

.................................................................................................................................................

**2.** ................................................................................................................................

.................................................................................................................................................

**3.** ................................................................................................................................

.................................................................................................................................................... [3]

# Communication of Ideas

**4** The area below represents a kitchen. Using **one-point perspective**, draw a rectangular block (representing a cooker) half way along the right-hand side.

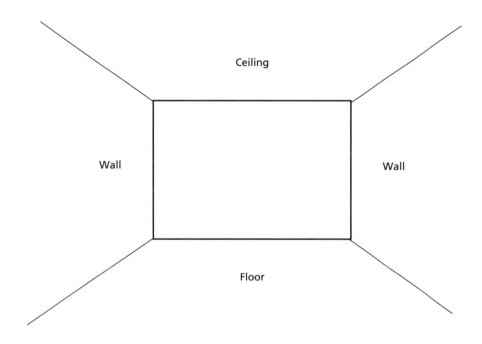

[4]

**5** State **three** different ways of modelling a design idea, and give a use for each.

**1.** ......................................................................................................................................................

Use ....................................................................................................................................................

............................................................................................................................................................

**2.** ......................................................................................................................................................

Use ....................................................................................................................................................

............................................................................................................................................................

**3.** ......................................................................................................................................................

Use ....................................................................................................................................................

............................................................................................................................................................

[6]

## Computer-Based Tools

6 This question is about computer-based tools.

Describe **three** ways that computer-based tools can be used to communicate design ideas.

**1.** ........................................................................................................................................................

........................................................................................................................................................

........................................................................................................................................................

........................................................................................................................................................

**2.** ........................................................................................................................................................

........................................................................................................................................................

........................................................................................................................................................

........................................................................................................................................................

**3.** ........................................................................................................................................................

........................................................................................................................................................

........................................................................................................................................................

........................................................................................................................................................ [6]

# Prototype Development

**7**  This question is about modelling and prototyping.

**7.1)**  Explain why designers produce prototypes.

_____

_____

_____

_____

_____

_____

_____

[4]

**7.2)**  Explain why card is a good material to use when producing early models of a design.

_____

_____

_____

_____

_____

_____

_____

[4]

Total Marks _____ / 41

# Energy Generation and Storage

Quick Recall Quiz

**You must be able to:**

- Describe how energy is generated and stored
- Explain the advantages and disadvantages of using renewable energy sources to power products and systems.

## Non-Renewable Energy Sources

- **Non-renewable energy sources** are sources that will eventually run out. The main examples are fossil fuels and nuclear power.

### Fossil Fuels

- **Fossil fuels** are formed from the remains of dead organisms over a very long period of time. Examples are coal, oil and natural gas.
- They are burned to create steam. This then turns turbines, which drive the generators that produce electricity.
- Burning fossil fuels releases carbon dioxide into the atmosphere, which can contribute to global warming.
- Fossil fuels will eventually run out, but many are currently in good supply. They are easy to find and allow the generation of huge amounts of electricity in a single location.

### Nuclear Power

- In **nuclear power** the steam needed to turn turbines and hence drive the generators is created using a nuclear reactor.
- Nuclear fission controls the reactor heat. This requires the use of uranium, which is a non-renewable resource.
- Making greater use of nuclear power means there is less need for fossil fuels.
- Although accidents are rare they can result in radioactive material being released into the environment. This can cause serious health problems for people living nearby.
- Strict procedures for disposal and storage of waste must be followed, as nuclear materials can stay hazardous for thousands of years.

Cooling towers at a nuclear power plant

> ### Key Point
>
> Renewable energy sources can replenish themselves quickly and so will not run out.

## Renewable Energy Sources

- **Renewable energy sources** are sustainable and will not run out. They are sources that can replenish themselves quickly. Examples include solar, wind, hydro-electrical, biomass and tidal.

### Solar

- Photovoltaic cells, or solar panels, collect and convert **solar energy**, light from the sun, into an electric current.
- Sunlight will not run out for billions of years, so there is an almost endless supply available.

Solar panels producing electricity for a house

- No waste products or greenhouse gases are emitted.
- Solar panels will produce less electricity when there is less sunlight. They produce no electricity at night.
- Installation and maintenance costs can be high.

### Wind

- Turbines that drive the generators are turned by the wind, harnessing **wind energy**.
- The amount of electricity that is produced depends on how much wind there is, so where they are positioned is crucial.
- No waste products or greenhouse gases are emitted.
- Some people feel that they are too noisy and do not like their visual impact on the landscape.

### Hydro-electrical

- To harness **hydro-electrical energy**, water is held in a reservoir and behind a dam. It is then released, turning a turbine which then generates electricity.
- Although clean and sustainable, creating a reservoir involves flooding large areas of land. This destroys habitats and forces people to move to new homes.
- Tidal is a form of hydro-electrical power that harnesses the energy from the tides of the sea to generate electricity.

### Biomass

- **Biomass** is fuel that is created from organic materials, such as crops, scrap wood and animal waste.
- Sources of biomass are readily available.
- Growing biomass crops produces oxygen and uses up carbon dioxide.
- It can be a very expensive way of producing fuel.

## Storing Energy

- **Batteries** convert chemical energy into electrical energy. Alkaline batteries work through the reaction between zinc and manganese dioxide. Rechargeable batteries are popular as they can be reused hundreds of times, thus reducing costs and the amount of waste that is sent to landfill sites.
- Kinetic pumped storage systems store energy in the form of water. Usually this is pumped from a lower reservoir to a higher reservoir. During times of high demand this can then be released through turbines to generate additional electricity.

Wind turbines

A pair of 1.5 V AA batteries

### Quick Test

1. How is electricity generated using fossil fuels?
2. What are the main sources of renewable energy?
3. What are the advantages of using renewable energy sources?

# Mechanical Systems 1

**You must be able to:**

- Describe the four types of motion
- Describe the basic principles of a lever
- Explain the different classes of lever.

## Types of Motion

- Most products and systems involve some form of motion.
- There are four types of motion:
  - **Rotating** motion means movement in a circle.
  - **Linear** motion goes in a straight line in one direction.
  - **Reciprocating** motion means moving backwards and forwards.
  - **Oscillating** motion means swinging backwards and forwards, like a pendulum.

## Principles of Levers

- **Levers** are a simple form of machine. They change the amount of **effort** or force needed to move a load.
- They consist of a rigid bar or beam that pivots around a fixed point called a **fulcrum**.
- A load is applied at one position on the lever.
- Effort is applied at another position on the lever. Sufficient effort results in movement of the lever about the fulcrum.
- Changing the distances between the fulcrum and either the load or the effort changes the amount of effort needed to move the load.
- There are three classes (or types) of lever.

### First-Order Lever

- In a first-order lever (also known as a first-class lever), the fulcrum is between the load and the effort.
- If the effort is further from the fulcrum than the load is, this results in a mechanical advantage. This means that the effort needed to move the lever is less than the load.
- The amount of mechanical advantage is proportional to the distance of the effort from the fulcrum and the distance of the load from the fulcrum.
- The distance that the effort and the load move is also proportional to the mechanical advantage.
- For example, if the effort is twice the distance from the fulcrum than the load is, the effort needed to move the load will be half of the value of the load. The distance that the effort will move will be double the distance that the load will move.
- Seesaws and scissors are examples of first-order levers.

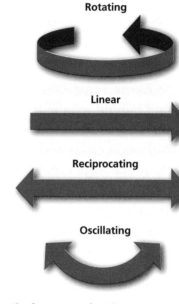

Rotating

Linear

Reciprocating

Oscillating

The four types of motion

### Key Point

There are four types of motion: rotating, linear, reciprocating and oscillating.

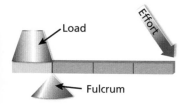

A first-order lever

First- and second-order levers can give a mechanical advantage, making it easier to move a load.

## Second-Order Lever

- In a second-order lever, the load is applied between the effort and the fulcrum.
- There is a mechanical advantage because the load is nearer the fulcrum than the effort.
- Nutcrackers and wheelbarrows are examples of second-order levers.

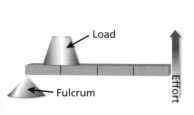

A second-order lever

## Third-Order Lever

- In a third-order lever, the effort is applied between the load and the fulcrum.
- The effort needed for movement is greater than the load, because the effort is nearer the fulcrum than the load. However, the amount of movement of the load is multiplied.
- Lifting a dumbbell is an example of a third-order lever: the load is the dumbbell, the fulcrum is the elbow and the effort is provided by the biceps muscle that attaches to the forearm between them.

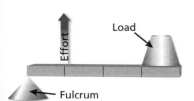

A third-order lever

**Key Words**

rotary
linear
reciprocating
oscillating
lever
effort
fulcrum

### Quick Test

1. What is the difference between reciprocating and oscillating motion?
2. What are the four common features of all levers?
3. Which type of lever does not give a mechanical advantage to the effort?

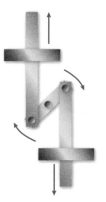

# Mechanical Systems 2

**You must be able to:**

- Describe how linkages, cams, gears and pulleys transfer motion
- Explain how these mechanical devices are used to change the magnitude and direction of forces.

**Energy and Mechanisms**

## Mechanical Devices

- Mechanical devices are used to transfer motion or force between mechanisms or to convert between different types of motion.

## Linkages

- **Linkages** are used to transfer motion between two positions. However, they can also act as levers (for example, in scissors).
- A push–pull linkage can reverse the direction of linear motion. It is also called a reversing linkage.
- A bell crank changes the direction of motion by an angle, for example 90°.

## Cams

- **Cams** are typically used to convert rotary motion to reciprocating motion.
- A follower is a rod that is moved as the cam rotates. This is normally connected to the object that is to be moved.
- A follower can only rise (go up), dwell (be held at the same height) or fall (go down). How long it spends doing each of these depends on the shape of the cam.
- Cams come in many different shapes, including eccentric circles, pear-shaped and snail-shaped. The different shapes give different amounts of time spent rising, dwelling or falling.
- A guide might be used to keep the follower in the correct place.
- Cams are used to provide the reciprocating movement of the needle in a sewing machine.

> **Key Point**
>
> Different mechanical devices are used to convert between different types of motion.

A push–pull linkage

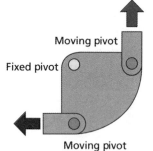

Bell crank changing the direction of motion by 90°

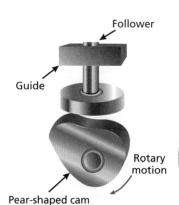

Pear-shaped cam

Rotary cam

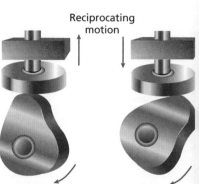

# Gears

- **Gears** have teeth that mesh with the teeth of other gears. Gears that work together must have teeth of the same size.
- Gears can change the speed or force of the motion they transfer. This is in proportion to the number of teeth they have. If a small gear turns a big gear with twice as many teeth, the big gear will rotate at half the speed of the small gear, but with twice the force.
- Spur gears transfer rotary motion. When using just two gears, the direction of movement is reversed. These are the most common gears used in gearboxes.
- Bevel gears change rotary motion through 90°. These are used in hand drills.
- A worm and worm wheel also change rotary motion through 90°. The worm gear is the driver (input) and has a single spiral tooth. This means that worm and worm wheels give a very large reduction in speed and a high torque (twisting force).
- A rack and pinion can be used to change rotary motion into linear motion. These are used in car steering or to move the base on a pillar drill up or down.

**Spur gears**

**Bevel gear**

**Worm and worm wheel**

**Rack and pinion**

Rack

Pinion

Types of gear

# Pulleys

- A **pulley** is a pair of grooved wheels with a belt running in the groove.
- This transfers rotary motion, with both wheels moving in the same direction. If the belt is crossed over, the two wheels will run in opposite directions.
- Like gears, pulleys can change the speed or force of the motion they transfer. This is in proportion to the radius of the pulley.
- The belt can move or stretch to adsorb shocks. However, if it is too loose or the force being transmitted is too high, the belt will slip and some (or even all) of the motion will not be transferred.
- Pulleys are often used in machines to transmit force from the motor to the tool, for example in drills, lathes and sewing machines.

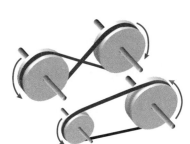

Pulleys

> ### Key Point
>
> In gears and pulleys, the speed and force transferred is proportional to the sizes of the two parts.

## Quick Test

1. Cams are used to change between which types of motion?
2. Name four types of gear.
3. What would be the effect of crossing over the belt in a pulley?

## Key Words

linkage
cam
gear
pulley

# Review Questions

## Research and Investigation

**1** **1.1)** Which of the following sentences best describes primary data?
Tick the correct box.

　　a. Data consisting of a collection of human measurements placed in tables. ☐

　　b. Data that comes from a mixture of first- and second-hand sources. ☐

　　c. Data that is freely available and obtained from other parties. ☐

　　d. Data that is obtained through first-hand investigation or research. ☐ [1]

**1.2)** Which of the following sentences best describes secondary data?
Tick the correct box.

　　a. Data consisting of a collection of human measurements placed in tables. ☐

　　b. Data that comes from a mixture of first- and second-hand sources. ☐

　　c. Data that is freely available and obtained from other parties. ☐

　　d. Data that is obtained through first-hand investigation or research. ☐ [1]

**1.3)** Which of the following sentences best describes anthropometric data?
Tick the correct box.

　　a. Data consisting of a collection of human measurements placed in tables. ☐

　　b. Data that comes from a mixture of first- and second-hand sources. ☐

　　c. Data that is freely available and obtained from other parties. ☐

　　d. Data that is obtained through first-hand investigation or research. ☐ [1]

# Briefs and Specifications

**2** Define each of the following.

Design brief

_____

_____

_____

_____

Design specification

_____

_____

_____

_____

Manufacturing specification

_____

_____

_____

_____

[6]

# Review Questions

## Exploring and Developing Ideas

**3** Explain in detail the steps taken when developing design ideas using an iterative process.

[9]

# Communication of Ideas

**4** Describe the purpose of an exploded view drawing and give an example of how it may be used.

[2]

**5** Describe the characteristics of an isometric drawing.

[2]

**6** The image below (in part **6.2**) is an orthographic projection of a simple product.

**6.1)** Circle the term that indicates the type of orthographic projection shown.

First angle        Second angle        Third angle        [1]

**6.2)** Label the different views.

i)

ii)                          iii)

i) _____  ii) _____  iii) _____  [3]

# Review Questions

## Computer-Based Tools

**7**  **7.1)** Tick the correct box. Presentation software is used for:

   **a.** Producing a bill of materials with calculations of cost. ☐

   **b.** Producing a simulation of an intended design for a product. ☐

   **c.** Producing a mathematical model of a product design. ☐

   **d.** Producing visual aids for a product presentation to a client. ☐  [1]

**7.2)** Tick the correct box. Spreadsheet software can be used for:

   **a.** Producing a bill of materials with calculations of cost. ☐

   **b.** Producing a simulation of an intended design for a product. ☐

   **c.** Producing an output file for use on a CAM machine. ☐

   **d.** Producing visual aids for a product presentation to a client. ☐  [1]

**7.3)** Tick the correct box. CAD software is often used for:

   **a.** Producing an audio presentation for a client. ☐

   **b.** Producing a simulation of an intended design for a product. ☐

   **c.** Producing a virtual environment for a client meeting. ☐

   **d.** Producing visual aids for a product presentation to a client. ☐  [1]

# Prototype Development

**8** Discuss the considerations that designers must take account of when developing prototypes.

[9]

# Practice Questions

## Energy Generation and Storage

**1** This question is about energy sources.

**1.1)** Give **two** specific examples of non-renewable energy sources.

1. .................................................................................................................................................

2. ................................................................................................................................................. [2]

**1.2)** Wind is an example of a renewable energy source. Give **two** other specific examples of renewable energy sources.

1. .................................................................................................................................................

2. ................................................................................................................................................. [2]

**1.3)** Explain **one** advantage and **one** disadvantage of using wind energy to power products.

Advantage ................................................................................................................................

.................................................................................................................................................

.................................................................................................................................................

.................................................................................................................................................

Disadvantage ..........................................................................................................................

.................................................................................................................................................

.................................................................................................................................................

.................................................................................................................................................
[4]

# Mechanical Systems

**2** State what is meant by each of the following types of motion.

**2.1)** Linear

.......................................................................................................................................... [1]

**2.2)** Rotating

.......................................................................................................................................... [1]

**2.3)** Reciprocating

.......................................................................................................................................... [1]

**2.4)** Oscillating

.......................................................................................................................................... [1]

**3** Two gears similar to those shown are being used to transfer motion in a mechanical device.

**3.1)** The input (driver) gear is turning clockwise. What is the direction of the output (driven) gear?

.......................................................................................................................................... [1]

**3.2)** Imagine that the input gear had 12 teeth and the output gear had 36 teeth.
Calculate the gear ratio.

..........................................................................................................................................

..........................................................................................................................................

..........................................................................................................................................

.......................................................................................................................................... [2]

**Total Marks** .............. / 15

# Properties of Materials

**You must be able to:**

- Explain the meanings of the properties of materials
- Describe the typical properties of different types of materials.

## Working Properties

- The working properties of a material are those that involve how the materials react to some form of applied force.
- **Strength** is the ability of a material to withstand a force or load that is applied to it. The strength will be different for different types of force applied to the material. These forces could be:
  - tension (pulling)
  - compression (squeezing)
  - torsion (twisting)
  - bending
  - shear (two parallel forces in opposite directions to each other).
- **Elasticity** is the ability of a material to return to its original shape when a force on it is removed.
- **Ductility** is the amount that a material can be permanently stretched or deformed when a force is applied to it.
- **Malleability** is the ability of a material for its shape to be permanently changed without breaking.
- **Hardness** is the ability of a material to resist wear or being scratched.
- **Toughness** is the ability of a material to not break when a force is applied to it suddenly. It is also known as impact resistance.

> ### Key Point
>
> Material properties have specific names. These can be used to compare or select materials for an application.

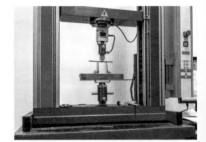

Machine to test tensile strength of material (resistance to pulling force)

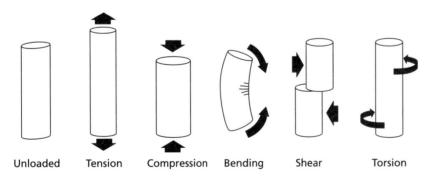

Unloaded    Tension    Compression    Bending    Shear    Torsion

Types of force

Samples of steel after tensile testing

# Physical Properties

- A physical property is a measurable characteristic of a material.
- **Density** is the mass of material per unit volume. This can be measured in kg m$^{-3}$ or g cm$^{-3}$.
- **Thermal conductivity** is the ability of a material to allow heat to pass through it. It is measured in watts per metre per Kelvin (W m$^{-1}$ K$^{-1}$).
- **Electrical conductivity** is the ability of a material to allow electricity to pass through it. A material with low electrical conductivity has high resistance.
- **Absorbency** is the ability of a material to draw in moisture.
- **Fusibility** is the ability of a material to be changed from a solid to a liquid by heat. This is important, for example, when joining materials by welding or soldering.

Hardness testing machine

## Typical Relative Properties of Different Types of Material

- The table compares the properties of different types of material. It only gives an indication of typical properties: specific named materials might have properties different to those stated.

> **Key Point**
>
> Types of material have different combinations of characteristic properties.

| Property | Timbers | Metals | Thermoforming Polymers | Thermosetting Polymers |
|---|---|---|---|---|
| Tensile strength | Low | High | Low to medium | Medium to high |
| Compressive strength | Medium | High | Low to medium | Low to medium |
| Hardness | Low to medium | High | Low to medium | Medium |
| Toughness | Medium | High | Low to medium | Medium |
| Malleability | Low | High | High | Low |
| Ductility | Low | Medium | High | Low |
| Elasticity | Low | Medium to high | Low | Low |
| Density | Low to medium | Medium to high | Low to medium | Low to medium |
| Fusibility | Low | High | High | Low |
| Absorbency | High | Low | Low | Low |
| Thermal conductivity | Low | High | Low | Low |
| Electrical conductivity | Low | High | Low | Low |

> **Key Words**
>
> strength
> elasticity
> ductility
> malleability
> hardness
> toughness
> density
>
> thermal conductivity
> electrical conductivity
> absorbency
> fusibility

> **Quick Test**
>
> 1. Name the five types of force that can be applied to a material.
> 2. Name three physical properties of material.
> 3. Explain the difference between elasticity and ductility.

# Materials: Paper and Board

**You must be able to:**

- Describe the characteristic properties and common uses of a variety of papers and boards
- Describe the standard sizes of paper
- Explain how paper and boards are converted into usable material.

## Types of Paper and Board

| Type | Characteristic Properties | Typical Uses |
|------|---------------------------|--------------|
| Layout and tracing paper | Relatively hard and translucent<br>Typically 50–90 **gsm** | Working drawings, tracing |
| Bleed-proof paper | Smooth and relatively hard<br>Resistant to inks and colours seeping through the paper, allowing clear, sharp images<br>Typically 70–150 gsm | Used with water-based and spirit-based felt-tip pens<br>Printed multi-coloured flyers and leaflets |
| Cartridge paper | Tough and lightly textured<br>Typically a very light cream colour<br>100–150 gsm | Drawing and painting<br>Printed flyers and leaflets |
| Grid paper | Printed square and isometric grids in different sizes<br>Typically 60–100 gsm | Quick sketches and model-making |
| Corrugated cardboard | Contains two or more layers of card with interlacing fluted inner section (adds strength without a significant weight increase)<br>Often made from recycled material; low cost<br>From 250 gsm upwards | General-purpose material for boxes and packaging |
| Duplex board (carton board) | White surfaces with grey fibres between<br>Tough and lightly textured<br>Lower cost than fully bleached card<br>May include additives to prevent moisture transfer and absorbance<br>230–420 gsm | Food packaging |
| Foil-lined board | Made by laminating aluminium foil to one side of cardboard, solid white board or duplex board<br>Insulating properties, can keep moisture in/out | Drinks cartons, ready-meal lids |
| Foam core board | Paper surfaces covering polystyrene centre<br>Typically 1.5–12 mm thick | Mounting of pictures, architectural models |
| Solid white board (bleached card) | Strong, high-quality, white board<br>Made from pure bleached wood pulp<br>200–400 gsm | Excellent for printing; book covers, expensive packaging |
| Inkjet card | Strong card; high-quality forms are often coated<br>Typically 240–280 gsm | Printing on inkjet printers; greetings cards and business cards |

> ### Key Point
>
> Different types of paper and card have different thicknesses and are suitable for different functions.

A roll of tracing paper

Inkjet card

# Standard Sizes and Forms

- Paper is available in sheet or rolls, often in a wide range of colours. Some paper products have more than one layer (or **ply**) of paper.
- Sheets of paper come in standard sizes, specified by an ISO (International Organization for Standardization) standard.
- A6 paper is the smallest size, measuring 105 × 148 mm; the area doubles with each size, up to A0 at 841 × 1189 mm.
- The weight of paper and card is specified in grams per square metre, referred to as gsm. In general, the higher the value of the gsm, the thicker the paper.
- Standard printer paper is generally around 80 gsm. Typically, card products are 200 gsm or more.

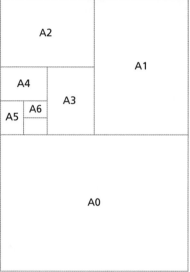

Paper sizes

# Source and Disposal

- Paper and card are made from cellulose fibres derived from wood and grasses. Chemicals are added to produce the required texture and surface finish.
- Wood pulp can be sourced from managed forests, where new trees are planted to replace those that are used. This helps to reduce the environmental impact.
- Most paper and card can be recycled at the end of its life by being processed and mixed with wood pulp. However, recycled paper cannot be used to make food packaging. If put into landfill, paper is **biodegradable**.
- Foil-lined board is a composite material and cannot be recycled.

**Key Point**

Paper and card can be recycled; however, composites combining other materials with paper cannot normally be recycled.

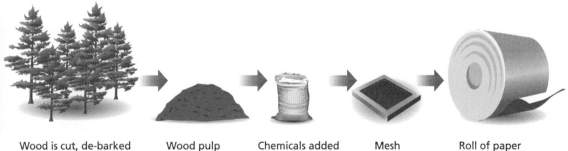

| Wood is cut, de-barked and turned into pulp | Wood pulp | Chemicals added (chalk and dye) | Mesh | Roll of paper |

Manufacturing process for paper

**Quick Test**

1. Which type of card is excellent for printing on?
2. What does gsm stand for?
3. Why can't recycled paper be used for carton board?

**Key Words**

gsm
ply
biodegradable

# Materials: Timber

Quick Recall Quiz

**You must be able to:**

- Explain the difference between hardwood and softwood
- Describe the characteristic properties and common uses of a variety of natural and manufactured timbers
- Explain how timber is converted into usable material.

## Natural Timber

- Timber is the general name for wood materials.
- Properties can vary according to the direction of the **grain**.
- At the end of its usable life, wood can be burnt as fuel or broken down into fibres for use in manufactured timbers. If put into landfill, wood is biodegradable.

## Hardwood

- **Hardwoods** come from deciduous trees, which shed their leaves each autumn.

Deciduous tree (oak)

| Hardwood | Characteristic Properties | Typical Uses |
|----------|---------------------------|--------------|
| Oak | Very strong and hard, but easy to work with<br>Open grained; light brown colour | High-quality furniture |
| Birch | Hard but easy to work with<br>Close, fine grain; pale, very light brown colour | Furniture and cabinets<br>Turned items |
| Ash | Tough and flexible<br>Open-grained, light creamy brown colour | Tool handles, sports equipment, wooden ladders |
| Mahogany | Fairly strong and durable<br>Some interlocking grain; pink to reddish-brown colour | High-quality furniture |
| Balsa | Soft: can be marked using a finger<br>Off-white to tan colour | Modelling |

## Softwood

- **Softwoods** come from coniferous trees.
- They maintain their foliage all year round, which is one reason why they typically grow faster than hardwood trees.
- They have a more open grain than hardwood trees and also typically cost less.
- Softwood from managed forests is a renewable resource: new trees are planted as each one is cut down.

Coniferous tree (pine)

| Softwood | Characteristic Properties | Typical Uses |
|----------|---------------------------|--------------|
| Pine | Fairly strong and durable, but easy to work with<br>Straight grained, light brown or yellowish in colour | Construction work and joinery, furniture |
| Larch | Tough, water resistant and durable<br>Grain is generally straight or spiralled<br>Heartwood ranges from yellow to medium brown colour; sapwood is nearly white | Boats and yachts, exterior cladding of buildings, interior panelling |
| Spruce | Strong and hard, but low resistance to decay<br>Straight grained with yellowish-white colour | General construction<br>Wooden aircraft frames |

# Standard Sizes and Forms

- The tree trunks are cut into planks in a sawmill. Plank sizes are limited by the sizes of the tree trunks available.
- Planks are available in a range of lengths, widths and thicknesses, either as rough sawn or planed square edge (PSE). PSE sizes are slightly smaller than rough sawn, as they have been planed to make them smooth.
- Wood may be seasoned. This means that it is dried before use to remove moisture, either in air or by gentle heating in a large kiln. This makes the wood less likely to distort or warp.
- Also available in a variety of standard sections called mouldings.

Trees in a forest after felling

Revise

**Key Point**

'Hardwood' and 'softwood' refer to the type of tree that the timber comes from, not the properties of the wood.

# Manufactured Timbers

- Also known as manufactured boards, these are made by gluing wood fibres or **veneers** together.
- The fibres can be waste materials from the cutting of natural timber.
- Properties are typically uniform as there is no grain.
- The top layer of most manufactured boards can be a veneer from a high-quality wood, to give a good appearance, or a plastic laminate for protection.
- Manufactured timber is made in very large sheets of consistent quality and not limited by the size of the trees. The most common sheet size is 2440 × 1220 mm (8 ft × 4 ft).
- Sheets are available in standard thicknesses; for example, 3, 6, 9, 12 mm, etc.

Wood mouldings

**Key Point**

Manufactured boards offer consistent properties and more of the tree is used than for wood.

| Manufactured Board | Description | Typical Uses | Appearance |
|---|---|---|---|
| Medium-density fibreboard (MDF) | Made from fine particles of timber, mixed with a bonding agent or glue and compressed. Smooth, even surface, easily machined | Furniture, interior panelling |  MDF |
| Plywood | Constructed from layers of veneer or plies; these are cut or shaved from timber, then glued together with the grain structure at 90° to each other. Interior and exterior grades available | Furniture making. Marine plywood is used for boat building | Plywood |
| Chipboard | Made from coarse particles (chips) of timber, mixed with a bonding agent or glue and compressed. Rough surface and uneven texture; often covered with a laminate of natural timber or a polymer such as melamine formaldehyde | Kitchen worktops | Chipboard  |

**Quick Test**

1. Name five types of hardwood.
2. Name three types of softwood.
3. Name three types of manufactured board.

**Key Words**

grain
hardwood
softwood
veneer

# Materials: Metals

**You must be able to:**

- Explain the difference between ferrous and non-ferrous metals
- Describe the characteristic properties and common uses of a variety of metals
- Explain how metal ore is converted into usable material.

## Making Metal

- Metal ore is extracted from the ground by mining or quarrying.
- The metal is refined from ore by large-scale industrial processes requiring a massive amount of energy. These may involve heat, chemical reactions to remove unwanted elements, or electrolysis.
- After refining, metals are typically melted and either cast into products or shaped into stock forms.
- They might be heat treated to modify their properties (e.g. metal can be annealed, which softens it and improves its malleability). Metals can be recycled by melting them down and reprocessing into new products.

Opencast quarrying of iron ore

Smelting of metal

## Ferrous Metals

- Ferrous metals contain iron.
- They are the most commonly used metals, with many applications.
- Typically they have a melting point of 1600°C or higher and most are silver-grey in colour.
- Most ferrous materials are prone to rusting and corrosion and can be picked up with a magnet (except stainless steel).

### Key Point

Ferrous metals have a huge variety of applications.

| Ferrous Metal | | Characteristic Properties | Typical Uses |
| --- | --- | --- | --- |
| Cast iron | | Good hardness and compressive strength, but poor tensile strength and brittle under tension | Engine blocks, cookware, piping |
| Low-carbon steel | | Tough, relatively low cost and easy to machine<br>Prone to corrosion | Car body panels, nuts and bolts, engine parts |
| High-carbon (tool) steel |  | Very strong and hard<br>More brittle and less ductile than low-carbon steel | Springs, high-tension wires |

## Non-Ferrous Metals

- Non-ferrous metals do not contain iron.
- They typically have good corrosion resistance, but they do tarnish.
- Non-ferrous materials are non-magnetic, so when sorting for recycling can be separated from ferrous materials using magnets.

| Non-ferrous Metal | Characteristic Properties | Typical Uses |
|---|---|---|
| Aluminium | Lighter than steel, but not as strong | Drinks cans, cooking pans, food packaging |
| Copper | Excellent conductor of heat and electricity | Electrical wiring, water pipes |
| Tin | Relatively soft and malleable Excellent corrosion resistance to water: used to plate steel containers to make 'tins' for food | Coating steel cans for corrosion resistance, alloying element in solder |
| Zinc | Hard and brittle, but becomes malleable between 100 and 150°C Relatively low melting point (419.5°C) | As a coating on steel (galvanising) to improve corrosion resistance; or as the anode in alkaline batteries |

# Common Alloys

- Most metals are used as **alloys**.
- An alloy is a mixture of two or more metals, created by melting the metals and adding them together. They can be either ferrous or non-ferrous depending upon the metals used.

| Alloy | Main Constituents | Characteristic Properties | Typical Uses |
|---|---|---|---|
| Brass  | Copper and zinc | Low friction Corrosion resistant Malleable | Locks, bearings, musical instruments |
| Stainless steel | Iron and chromium, with a small amount of carbon | Tough, strong and hard Difficult to machine Corrosion resistant | Kitchen equipment, medical instruments |
| High-speed steel (HSS) | Iron with small amounts of carbon, tungsten, molybdenum, vanadium and chromium | A sub-set of tool steels (see p. 66). Very hard, even at high temperatures, allowing HSS tools to cut faster even when heated by friction Strong but brittle with low ductility | Power saw blades, drill bits, files, chisels, woodturning tools |

# Stock Forms

- Metals are available in a wide variety of standard shapes, including sheet, rod, round or square bar, and tube. Each shape is typically available in a wide range of lengths, widths, thicknesses and diameters (where applicable).
- It requires much energy to reform metal so designers try to use standard shapes and sizes, or use a size that requires the least machining.
- Metal ingots can also be melted down and cast into complex shapes.

**Quick Test**

1. What is the meaning of the term 'alloy'?
2. Name three metal alloys.
3. What are the typical properties of zinc?

**Key Words**

ferrous metal
non-ferrous metal
alloy

# Materials: Polymers

Quick Recall Quiz

**You must be able to:**

- Explain how polymers are converted into usable material
- Explain the difference between thermoforming and thermosetting polymers
- Describe the properties and uses of a variety of polymers
- Describe the forms in which polymers are available
- Explain what happens to polymers at the end of their usable life.

## Making Polymers

- **Polymers** are made from chains of similar small chemical units, called monomers. The process of attaching the monomers together is called polymerisation.
- Most commonly used polymers are **synthetic**. They are manufactured from carbon-based fossil fuels such as oil.
- The oil is refined using industrial-scale chemical processes. It is separated into the different chemicals it contains by **fractional distillation**. The chemicals needed to make the polymers are broken down into the monomers by a process called **cracking**.
- Fossil fuels are a **finite resource**. Extracting and transporting them has an impact on the environment.
- Some polymers will break down slowly and become weaker when exposed to the ultraviolet (UV) light in sunlight. To resist this degradation, chemical stabilisers may be added to the material.
- Synthetic polymers are not normally biodegradable.

Drilling for oil and gas at sea

> ### Key Point
>
> Most synthetic polymers are made from fossil fuels, a non-renewable resource.

Polymer recycling symbols

## Thermosetting Polymers

- **Thermosetting polymers** cannot soften when heated but may char. Their polymer chains are interlinked with permanent chemical bonds.
- They are commonly available in liquid form (as resins) or as powders. These must be cured (heated) or reacted with chemicals to create the polymer.
- At the end of their usable life, thermosetting polymers typically end up being disposed to landfill.

| Thermosetting Polymer | Characteristic Properties | Typical Uses |
|---|---|---|
| Epoxy resin | Made by mixing a chemical resin with a hardener <br> Hard but brittle unless reinforced; resist chemicals well | Printed circuit boards, adhesive (Araldite) |
| Polyester resin | Made by mixing a chemical resin with a hardener <br> Often reinforced with glass fibre to form the composite glass-reinforced polyester (GRP) <br> Stiff, hard, but brittle unless laminated | Car bodies, boats |
| Urea formaldehyde | Hard, strong, stiff, excellent insulator but brittle | Plug sockets, electrical switches, door handles |
| Melamine formaldehyde | Heat resistant, hard, resists some chemicals and stains | Laminates for kitchen worktops |
| Phenol formaldehyde | Made by a chemical reaction between phenol and formaldehyde; hard with high strength, high strength-to-weight ratio and excellent flame resistance | Snooker balls, laboratory countertops, coatings and adhesives |

# Thermoforming Polymers

- **Thermoforming polymers** are also known as thermoplastics. They soften when they are heated and can be shaped when hot. When cooled they harden in the new shape, but can be reshaped again if reheated.
- Most thermoforming polymers are available in sheets of standard thickness (gauge), for example 1.5, 2 mm, etc. Some are also available as films, foam or rods in a range of lengths, widths and, if applicable, diameters. They are also available as pellets or granules for injection moulding and as powders for dip-coating.
- Thermoforming polymer products are commonly marked to identify which type of polymer they are made from.
- If sorted into their different types, thermoforming polymers can be recycled.

Polymer granules used for injection moulding

| Thermoforming Polymer | Characteristic Properties | Typical Uses |
|---|---|---|
| PET (polyethylene terephthalate) | Transparent, commonly used for vacuum forming or blow moulding Softens at about 80°C | Drinks bottle, food packaging |
| HDPE (high-density polyethylene) | Strong, stiff Softens at about 130°C | Pipes, bowls, buckets |
| PVC (polyvinylchloride) | Stiff, hard-wearing Softens at about 100–125°C | Pipes, packaging, chemical tanks |
| HIPS (high-impact polystyrene) | Light, strong Softens at about 90°C Commonly used in schools for vacuum forming | Packaging |
| PP (polypropylene) | Low density, tough and flexible Softens at about 140–150°C | Ropes, carpets, packaging |
| PMMA (polymethyl-methacrylate) | Known by the trade names Acrylic and Perspex Hard wearing, can be transparent or coloured Softens between 85–165°C depending on grade | Display signs, plastic windows, baths |

 **Key Point**

Thermoforming polymers can be reshaped and recycled. Thermosetting polymers cannot.

## Quick Test

1. What are synthetic polymers commonly made from?
2. In which forms are thermosetting polymers typically available?
3. Name three typical uses of polypropylene.

**Key Words**

polymer
synthetic
fractional distillation
cracking
finite resource
thermosetting polymer
thermoforming polymer

# Materials: Textiles

**You must be able to:**

- Explain how fabric is constructed from fibres
- Explain the difference between natural, synthetic and blended fibres
- Describe the characteristic properties and common uses of a variety of textiles.

## Fibres and Fabrics

- Textiles is a general term used to describe any product that is made from a fabric.
- Fabric is made from fibres. These fine, hair-like particles range from short lengths (staple fibres) to continuous filaments.
- Individual fibres are weak, so they are spun and twisted together to produce **yarn**.
- Fibres and fabrics may be treated with flame retardants. These reduce the risk of combustion and fire hazards.

Weft-knitted fabric

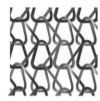

Warp-knitted fabric

Non-woven fabric
Fabric construction

## Fabric Construction

- **Knitted** fabrics are made from yarns in a series of interlocking loops. Loops may be arranged in different ways, called weft and warp. Knitted fabrics are warm and stretchy (elastic).
- **Woven** fabrics are constructed from interlaced yarns. The fabric has a grain due to the direction of the threads. It is strongest along the straight grain of the fabric when the weave is close and firm, but lacks elasticity.
- Woven fabric has a **selvedge** – an edge that will not fray. However, the fabric will fray easily when cut.
- Non-woven fabrics (such as felt) are made from entangled raw fibres, rather than yarns.
- Non-woven fabrics may be made by using chemicals to mat the fibres together, with heat to bond the fibres or by stitching the fibres in layers and interlocking them.

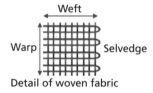

Detail of woven fabric

**Key Point**

Fabrics are constructed from fibres by knitting, weaving or non-woven methods.

## Natural and Synthetic Fibres

### Natural Fibres

- **Natural fibres** come from animals or plants.
- Animal fibres include wool, silk, alpaca, angora, camel hair, cashmere, mohair and vicuña.
- Plant fibres include cotton, linen, jute, hemp and ramie.
- Natural fibres are biodegradable.

Group of cocoons and a silkworm

## Synthetic Fibres

- **Synthetic fibres** are made by people, typically from oil or chemicals.
- Oil is a fossil fuel. It is a finite resource, so once it is used it is not naturally replaced quickly. Extracting and transporting oil can cause environmental damage or pollution.
- The oil is processed using large-scale industrial processes to extract the chemicals needed to make the fibres.
- Synthetic fibres are not typically biodegradable.

Offshore oil platform

| Natural Fibre | Characteristic Properties | Typical Uses |
|---|---|---|
| Cotton | A vegetable/cellulose fibre, from the ripened seeds of the cotton plant<br>Strong, durable, absorbent, creases easily | Denim, calico, flannelette, gabardine<br>Underwear, shirts and blouses, T-shirts, jeans |
| Wool | An animal/protein fibre, from the fleeces of sheep<br>Warm, soft, absorbent, crease resistant | Felt, flannel, gabardine<br>Jumpers, suits, dresses, carpets |
| Silk | An animal/protein fibre, from the cocoon of the silk moth<br>Smooth, lustrous and strong | Chiffon, organza, crepe, velvet<br>Dresses, shirts, ties |

| Synthetic Fibre | Characteristic Properties | Typical Uses |
|---|---|---|
| Polyamide (Nylon) | Produced from two different chemical monomers<br>Strong, durable, warm, crease resistant | Tights and stockings, sportswear, upholstery, carpets |
| Polyester | Produced from coal and oil<br>Strong, durable, elastic, crease resistant | Sportswear |
| Elastane (Lycra) | Produced from polyurethane chemicals<br>High extension and elasticity (stretch)<br>Used to improve comfort and appearance of the garment when added to other fabrics | Sportswear, underwear, socks, suits |

# Blended Fibres

- Blended fibres use a mixture of different types of fibre. They combine the properties of different fibres.
- One of the best known is polycotton, which has the absorbency of cotton and quick-drying properties of polyester.

# Availability and Use of Textiles

- Most fabrics are available in stock forms. They are normally sold by roll size, width, weight and ply (the number of layers of the fabric).
- When cutting textile products from fabric, consideration should be given to the layout of the pattern to minimise waste material.
- Textile products can often be reused or recycled. However, many are incinerated or go to landfill.

Polycotton towels

## Quick Test

1. Name three different types of fabric construction.
2. Name three natural fibres.
3. What is polyester made from?

# New Materials

**You must be able to:**

- Describe the characteristics of a variety of new materials
- Explain what is meant by a smart material and a composite material
- List specific technical textiles, and modern, smart and composite materials, and their typical uses.

Quick Recall Quiz

## Modern Materials

- New or improved manufacturing processes have led to the development of titanium alloys with improved properties, **metal foams** and **graphene**.
- Often developments in materials involve altering a material to perform a particular function. One way to do this is coating the material with a **nanomaterial**. Other examples include:
  - coating metals to improve the properties of their surface, such as corrosion resistance or hardness
  - changing the physical state of materials, such as creating the liquid crystals used to make liquid crystal displays (LCDs).

> **Key Point**
>
> Materials with improved properties are constantly being developed.

## Metal Foams

- Metal foams are made from metal containing gas-filled pores. They look like a sponge made from metal.
- They have the physical properties of the metal, but can be 75–95% lighter in weight.
- Their main current uses are for sound damping and crash-resistant structures in vehicles.

## Graphene

- Graphene is a form of carbon. Its atoms are arranged hexagonally in a flat 2D layer, just one atom thick.
- It is about 200 times stronger than steel, flexible, transparent and conducts heat and electricity well.
- Potential applications include solar cells, touch panels and smart windows for phones.

Structure of graphene

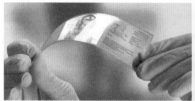

Potential graphene application: a flexible screen

## Nanomaterials

- Nanomaterials are made up of particles that are less than 100 nanometres in size.
- Nanomaterial coatings for glass and fabrics can repel dirt or water, giving 'self-cleaning' properties.

## Smart Materials

- Smart materials have a property that changes in response to an external stimulus. This change is reversible if the stimulus changes again.

> **Key Point**
>
> Smart materials have a property that changes when an external stimulus changes.

- The external stimulus could be, for example, temperature, light, moisture, stress or pH.
- Shape memory alloys change to their original shape when they are heated. They are used for spectacle frames, which if accidentally bent can be heated and returned to their original shape.
- Thermochromic pigments change colour in response to temperature. They are used for flexible thermometers and food packaging.
- Photochromic pigments change colour in response to light levels. They are used for glasses that get darker in bright light.

Changes to dark in sunlight

Photochromic lenses in glasses

# Composites

- **Composites** combine the properties of two or more materials.
- Weight for weight, a carbon-fibre-reinforced composite can have up to six times the strength of steel.
- Unlike an alloy, the materials in a composite are not mixed at a chemical level; if you look at the material under a microscope you can see the separate materials in contact with each other.
- Common composites include:
  - glass-reinforced polyester (GRP) and fibreglass, used in car body building and repair and boat hulls
  - carbon-reinforced polyester (CRP) used to make tent poles, high-performance bicycles and sports equipment.
- As the materials cannot easily be separated, composites cannot normally be recycled. At the end of their usable life they are normally disposed of in landfill.

Sir Bradley Wiggins riding a bicycle made from composite materials in the Tour de France

> **Key Point**
>
> Composites combine the properties of two or more materials.

# Technical Textiles

- **Technical textiles** are manufactured for performance properties rather than visual appearance. They are made from fibres spun from materials with the required properties and woven into fabric.
- This includes fabrics designed to provide protection from injury or hazardous environments, such as:
  - Kevlar in body armour provides protection from weapon impact
  - fire-resistant fabric used in clothing worn by firefighters, to protect them from the flames of a burning building.
- Conductive fibres allow circuits to be incorporated into fabrics. These may be weaved or knitted into another fabric, or applied by printing or layering. These can be used to make temperature controlled clothing or to integrate lights into emergency clothing.
- Microfibres incorporating micro-encapsulation – such as woven polyester with tiny capsules embedded in the fibre – are used for socks and underwear that reduce body odour, or anti-bacterial medical textiles.

Policeperson in body armour

> **Key Words**
>
> metal foam
> graphene
> nanomaterials
> composite
> technical textile

> **Quick Test**
>
> 1. Which chemical element is graphene made from?
> 2. What size are the particles in nanomaterials?
> 3. Name two composite materials.

# Standard Components

**You must be able to:**

- Explain why standard components are used
- List standard components used with a variety of different materials.

## Stock Forms

- Stock forms are standard shapes and sizes in which materials are available. These vary for different materials and are listed on pages 94–103.
- To minimise effort, energy needs, waste and cost, designers normally try to use either a stock form or the closest size that requires the smallest amount of processing.

## Reasons for Using Standard Components

- Some types of component are used in many different products.
- These include fasteners and fixings to hold materials together, electrical components and mechanical parts.
- There are companies that have production lines dedicated to just making these **standard components**. This means they can:
  - buy materials in bulk, getting lower prices
  - divide the equipment cost across millions of parts
  - automate the processes
  - use labour efficiently
  - ensure that the consistency and quality of the products is maintained.
- The standard parts can then be bought at low cost by whoever needs them.
- The parts are normally available in a range of standard sizes. Designers normally take this into consideration when designing new products.

## Types of Standard Component

> **Key Point**
>
> Standard components are parts that are used in many different products.

> To make these parts in small quantities can be very expensive, due to the time and equipment required. For example: making one staple to attach some sheets of paper together would require a piece of material to be bought, the tools to cut it and bend it, and the time to make it.

> **Key Point**
>
> It is much cheaper to buy a standard component than to make a small quantity of the part.

| | | | |
|---|---|---|---|
| • Used with paper and boards:<br>  – clips<br>  – fasteners, for example plastic rivets, sticky tape<br>  – binders. | <br>Paper fasteners | <br>Plastic binder |  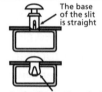<br>Plastic rivets<br>Two parts of the clic rivet<br>The base of the slit is straight<br>As the clic rivet is pushed in, the slit widens to hold it in place |
| • Used with timber:<br>  – hinges<br>  – brackets<br>  – screws<br>  – nails<br>  – handles, drawer runners and knock-down fittings. | <br>Door hinge | 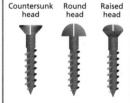<br>Countersunk head  Round head  Raised head<br>Types of screw | 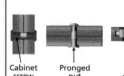 <br>Cabinet screw  Pronged nut  Cross dowel  Modesty block<br>Knock-down fitting |

- Used with polymers:
  - caps
  - fasteners
  - nuts, bolts and washers.

Plastic nuts and bolts

Plastic caps

- Used with fibres and fabrics:
  - zips
  - buttons
  - poppers and press studs
  - Velcro
  - decorative items, such as embroidered decals, sequins and beads.

Zips

Buttons

Press stud

Velcro

- Used with metals:
  - nuts, bolts and washers
  - rivets
  - hinges.

Hexagonal-headed bolt
Washer
Nut

Bolt, washer and nut

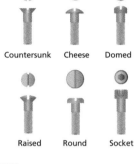

Countersunk   Cheese   Domed

Raised   Round   Socket

Screws

**Rivet heads**

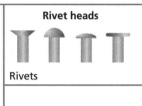

Rivets

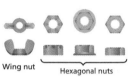

Wing nut   Hexagonal nuts

Nuts and bolts

Washers

- Electrical components used in control systems and circuits:
  - resistors
  - capacitors
  - diodes, including LEDs
  - transistors and drivers
  - microcontrollers
  - switches
  - motors.

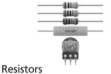

Resistors

**Microcontroller**

Microcontroller

Capacitors

Diodes

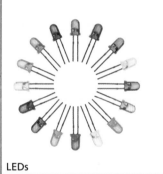

LEDs

- Mechanical components:
  - levers
  - linkages
  - gears
  - cams
  - pulleys
  - belts.

Metal gears

Plastic gears

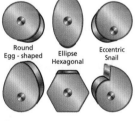

Round
Egg - shaped   Ellipse
Hexagonal   Eccentric
Snail

Cams

Pulleys and belts

## Quick Test

1. Name three standard components that attach metal parts together.
2. Name a type of standard component that is used with wood, metal and polymer.
3. Name four standard mechanical components.

**Key Words**

**standard component**

# Finishing Materials

**You must be able to:**

- Explain the purpose of surface treating and finishing materials
- Describe how surface treatments and finishing techniques are applied to a range of materials.

Quick Recall Quiz

## Purpose of Finishing

- The main reasons for finishing materials are to improve function or aesthetics.
- Functional considerations include durability and added resistance to overcome environmental factors. For example, painting wood to be used on a garden gate helps to make it water resistant.

> **Key Point**
>
> Finishing a material can improve its aesthetics, durability and resistance to damage.

## Metal-Based Materials

- Coating
  - Dip-coating involves blowing air through a powder to make it behave like a liquid, dipping the metal in the fluid and heating it to form a smooth finish.
  - Powder coating is a more sophisticated version of dip-coating where a powder is sprayed onto the metal. The powder and object are electrically charged to attract an even coat and then heated.
- Galvanising
  - Metal, often mild steel, is dipped into a bath of molten zinc.

Metals being powder coated in an industrial environment

## Polymers

- The main finishing technique for plastics is **polishing**.
  - Hard plastics such as acrylic are often polished on their cut edges. Polishing also removes fine scratches.
  - Polishing includes cutting the surface of the material until it is very smooth. Abrasive liquids can be applied to aid in this process.
  - Waxes or non-abrasive liquids can be used to fill in any subsequent gaps in the polymer.
- Vinyl decals can be used to add lettering and decoration to plastics.
- Plastics can also be printed onto. This is a highly specialised process.

## Timber-Based Materials

- Painting
  - Paints can be oil-, water- or solvent-based. They can be applied with a brush or sprayed onto the material.

Timber being painted

- Paints are used to both protect and decorate woods, and are available in a huge range of different colours.
- **Varnishing**
  - Polyurethane varnish is a tough, heat-proof and waterproof finish available in different colours.
  - It is usually applied in three coats with a brush. It can then be smoothed with fine glasspaper.
- Tanalising
  - Tanalising is a pressure treatment used to preserve wood.
  - Wood is placed into a closed cylinder and a vacuum is created. Pressure is then applied, which forces the preservative deep into the material.

## Textile-Based Materials

- Block and screen printing are the main printing methods used for textile-based materials.
- Textile-based materials can be dyed by hand or by machine. Continuous or batch dyeing techniques are used in many industrial applications.
- Stain-resistant finishes can also be applied.

## Papers and Boards

- Printing
  - The main printing processes for papers and boards are screen printing and block printing.
  - Lithography, flexography, letterpressing and gravure printing methods are used in commercial paper- and board-based products.
- **Embossing**
  - Steel dies are used to press a shape onto the material.
  - This gives a tactile effect and improves the visual look of the product.
- Ultraviolet varnishing
  - Ultraviolet (UV) varnishing involves applying a glossy coating to the surface of the paper or board, which is then immediately dried using UV light.

## Electronic and Mechanical Systems

- Printed circuit boards (PCBs) can be lacquered. This provides a waterproof protective layer for the tracks and pads of the PCB.
- Gears and other moving mechanical parts can be lubricated. This reduces the effects of friction, such as heat and noise.

Varnish being applied to a piece of wood

**Key Point**

Screen and block printing methods are commonly used when working with textile-based materials and paper and boards.

Mechanical parts, such as gears, can be lubricated to reduce the effects of friction

### Quick Test

1. What are the main reasons for finishing materials?
2. What is the main way of finishing plastics?
3. What does embossing result in?
4. Why are mechanical parts lubricated?

**Key Words**

polishing
varnishing
embossing
PCB lacquering

# Selection of Materials

**You must be able to:**

- Describe a wide range of factors that can influence the choice of material for a product
- Explain the important properties required by commercial products.

## Functionality and Choice of Material

- The material must have **functionality**: the mechanical and physical properties needed by the application for which it was designed.
- Designers will also consider the ease of working: how easily the product can be manufactured from the material.
- In addition, designers and customers may have a wide variety of other requirements that the products must meet.

## Factors Affecting Material Selection

- **Aesthetics** is how an object appeals to the five senses. Aesthetic properties include the surface finish and texture (whether the material is rough or smooth to touch, hard or soft) and the colour.
- Environmental considerations may include whether the product is made from recycled or reused materials and whether it is recyclable.
- Availability of materials: how easy these are to locate and buy, including whether they are available in standard stock forms.
- Cost: whether parts can be bought in bulk, at a discount.
- Social factors, such as social responsibility. For example, customer preferences for not using material sources from certain countries for political reasons.
- Ethical considerations, for example:
  - only using fair trade products, and not using parts made by workers who have been treated unfairly; for example, underage workers working in a sweat shop
  - only using material from ethical sources such as wood certified by the Forestry Stewardship Council (FSC) to be **sustainable**, where replacement trees are planted for each one used.
- Cultural factors, such as fashion.

## Properties Required in Commercial Products

- The table illustrates some of the important properties that may be considered when selecting the materials to manufacture the listed commercial products.

| Key Point |
| --- |
| Selecting which material to use is not just about the material properties: there are other things to consider as well. |

Metals are available in a wide variety of shapes and sizes

Recycling symbol

Ethical decisions

| Type of Material | Commercial Product | Examples of Important Properties |
|---|---|---|
| Paper and boards | Flyers and leaflets | Ability to be printed<br>Cost |
| | Food packaging | Absorbency, to prevent spoilage of contents or damage to the packaging<br>Ability to be printed, to give aesthetic appeal<br>Cost |
| Timber-based materials | Traditional timber children's toys | Aesthetics: colour and texture that appeal to children<br>Absorbency and resistance to corrosion, in case put in child's mouth<br>Toughness, to resist impacts or being dropped<br>Hardness, to resist being scratched or damaged in use |
| | Flat-pack furniture | Toughness, to resist impacts<br>Hardness, to resist being scratched or damaged in use<br>Cost |
| Metals and alloys | Cooking utensils (pans) | Thermal conductivity, to allow heat through<br>Absorbency and resistance to corrosion, to resist tainting the contents<br>Malleability for ease of manufacture<br>Hardness to avoid being scratched or worn when in use<br>Density, lightweight to lift easily |
| | Hand tools | Strength<br>Toughness, to resist impact if hit or dropped<br>Malleability, ability to be made into the shape of the tool (as material is very hard and may be difficult to form) |
| Polymers | Seating | Compressive strength to support the person sitting on it<br>Absorbency and resistance to corrosion, to resist damage by rain if used outside<br>Density, lightweight so can be lifted easily and put away |
| | Electrical fittings | Electrical conductivity: insulating to protect the user from the electrical circuit inside it<br>Toughness, so that it doesn't break if accidentally knocked, causing safety issues |
| Textile-based materials | Sportswear | Aesthetics: colour and texture that appeal to the user<br>Elasticity/stretchiness to provide a good fit/shape<br>Density, lightweight to avoid additional load on wearer |
| | Furnishings | Aesthetics: colour and texture that appeal to the user<br>Hardwearing so it lasts a long time<br>Non-flammable, so that it doesn't burn |
| Electronic and mechanical systems | Motor vehicles | Toughness so it doesn't break on impact in an accident<br>Density: lightweight to reduce fuel requirements<br>Absorbency and resistance to corrosion, so that it doesn't stop working in wet weather<br>Hardness of mechanical parts, so they last a long time before wearing out |
| | Domestic appliances (e.g. fridges, washing machines) | Absorbency and resistance to corrosion, so that it isn't damaged by the materials, water or food that contact it in use.<br>Strength, to support whatever is put into it and to resist damage if someone sits on it!<br>Electrical conductivity: it should insulate the circuitry to prevent electric shocks to the user |

## Quick Test

1. Name six types of need that a material may have to satisfy.
2. State two aesthetic properties that may be considered.
3. List two important properties for an electrical fitting made from polymer.

## Key Words

functionality
aesthetics
sustainable

# Working with Materials

Quick Recall Quiz

**You must be able to:**

- Explain why reinforcement is used in products
- Describe how the properties of a material can be enhanced
- Describe a range of examples of how product designs can be modified to improve the performance of a product.

## Meeting the Properties Needed by a Product

- Sometimes a preferred material can meet most of the requirements for a product or application, but not all of them. For example, it may have the strength needed and be low cost, but prone to corrosion.
- The properties of individual materials can often be modified to make them more suitable for specific applications.
- Alternatively, sometimes the design of the product can be modified so that the product can satisfy the requirements using the material.

## Examples of How Material Properties can be Modified

- Additives can be added to paper and board to prevent moisture transfer, for example in food packaging.
- The risk of timber warping can be reduced by seasoning (drying to remove moisture). This also results in a small increase in the hardness and strength of the timber.
- Annealing can be used to increase the malleability of metal. This involves heating the metal and allowing the grains in the microstructure to grow, which results in a small reduction in the hardness of the material.
- The surface of aluminium products can be anodized to improve hardness.
- Some polymers degrade when exposed to ultraviolet (UV) light for a long time; for example, PVC window frames can become brittle after being exposed to sunlight for several years. This can be avoided by mixing in stabilisers to resist UV degradation when the polymer is made.
- Flame retardants may be added to fabrics used in textile products, for example furniture covers or the protective clothing worn by firefighters. This reduces fire hazards by making the fabric more difficult to set on fire.
- Photosensitive board can be used to make PCBs for electronic circuits. The required circuit board design is masked to protect

### Key Point

The properties of some materials can often be enhanced to make them more suitable for specific applications.

### Key Point

The method used to enhance the properties of a product depends upon the type of product, what it is made from and what properties are needed.

Red anodized aluminium cycling hub

Firefighter

it from light. The board is then placed in light, after which it is dipped in chemicals to remove the unmasked areas of copper on the board. This leaves the tracks for the circuit design.

# Reinforcing the Design to Enhance Performance

- Products may need to be reinforced, stiffened or made more flexible so that they can achieve the properties that are needed from them.
- Compared to using a stronger or thicker material for the whole product, **reinforcement** allows just the part of the product that needs greater strength or stiffness to be enhanced. This means that the overall product can be lower cost or lighter in weight, or that some areas can be left with greater flexibility.
- There are many different ways to reinforce structures. The type of reinforcement used will depend upon the type of product being reinforced, the material that it is made from and the properties that are needed.

# Methods of Reinforcement

- Bending, folding and lamination can all be used to increase the effective thickness of material and the stiffness of a structure. These can be used with most sheet materials, such as paper and card, metal and fabrics.
- **Webbing** is ribs of material, normally located on the inside of a product. The ribs are long, raised pieces of material which increase the stiffness of the product. Ribs can be formed by adding extra material or by pressing or moulding the shape into the surface.
- **Interfacing** is used in fabric products. It involves adding extra layers of material to a textile product to increase its strength or make it more rigid. It is often used in shirt collars to make them stiff. It is normally used on the unseen or 'wrong' side of fabrics, for instance where buttonholes will be sewn.

Laminating paper

Plastic webbing adding stiffness to a battery casing

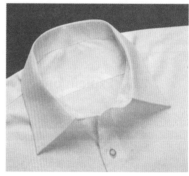

Shirt collar with added stiffness from interfacing

## Quick Test

1. Give one reason for annealing metal.
2. Name three methods used to increase the effective thickness of a material in a product.
3. Describe what is meant by 'webbing' in a product.

## Key Words

reinforcement
webbing
interfacing

# Review Questions

## Energy Generation and Storage

**1** This question is about energy generation and storage.

**1.1)** Explain **two** advantages of using rechargeable batteries instead of non-rechargeable batteries for storing energy.

**1.** ................................................................................................................................................

................................................................................................................................................

................................................................................................................................................

................................................................................................................................................

**2.** ................................................................................................................................................

................................................................................................................................................

................................................................................................................................................

................................................................................................................................................

[4]

**1.2)** Explain **one** advantage and **one** disadvantage of using biomass to power products.

Advantage ....................................................................................................................................

................................................................................................................................................

................................................................................................................................................

................................................................................................................................................

Disadvantage ...............................................................................................................................

................................................................................................................................................

................................................................................................................................................

................................................................................................................................................

[4]

# Mechanical Systems

**2** **2.1)** Give an example of a product that acts as a first-order lever.

.................................................................................................................... [1]

**2.2)** A second-order lever is giving a mechanical advantage of 3.

Calculate the effort needed to move a load of 24 newtons.

....................................................................................................................

....................................................................................................................

....................................................................................................................

.................................................................................................................... [2]

**2.3)** Explain the relationship between the effort and load in a third-order lever.

....................................................................................................................

....................................................................................................................

....................................................................................................................

.................................................................................................................... [2]

**3** For each of the following, name a mechanical device which can be used to:

**3.1)** Reverse the direction of a linear movement

.................................................................................................................... [1]

**3.2)** Transfer rotary movement through 90°

.................................................................................................................... [1]

**3.3)** Convert rotary movement to reciprocating movement

.................................................................................................................... [1]

**3.4)** Convert rotary movement into linear motion.

.................................................................................................................... [1]

**Total Marks** .................... / 17

## Properties of Materials

1 State the meaning of the following properties.

1.1) Tensile strength

.......................................................................................................................................................

....................................................................................................................................................... [1]

1.2) Density

.......................................................................................................................................................

....................................................................................................................................................... [1]

## Materials: Paper and Board

2 Using notes and/or sketches, describe the processes involved in converting paper from its raw material to a finished product.

[6]

## Materials: Timber

**3** **3.1)** **i)** Name a softwood.

............................................................................................................................................... [1]

**ii)** Give a typical use for this softwood.

...............................................................................................................................................

............................................................................................................................................... [1]

**iii)** Explain why this softwood is an appropriate choice for this application.

...............................................................................................................................................

...............................................................................................................................................

...............................................................................................................................................

............................................................................................................................................... [2]

**3.2)** **i)** Name a hardwood.

............................................................................................................................................... [1]

**ii)** Give a typical use for this hardwood.

...............................................................................................................................................

............................................................................................................................................... [1]

**iii)** Explain why this hardwood is an appropriate choice for this application.

...............................................................................................................................................

...............................................................................................................................................

...............................................................................................................................................

............................................................................................................................................... [2]

**4** Name two stock forms in which timber is available.

**1.** ............................................................................................................................................... [1]

**2.** ............................................................................................................................................... [1]

# Practice Questions

## Materials: Metals

5  Using notes and/or sketches, describe the processes involved in converting metals from their raw materials to finished products.

[4

6  Complete the table, filling in the missing information about metals. The first line has been completed as an example.

| Type | Name | Characteristics | Typical Use |
|---|---|---|---|
| Ferrous | Low-carbon steel | Tough, prone to corrosion | Car body panels |
| a) | Aluminium | Not as strong as steel but lighter | b) |
| Ferrous alloy | c) | Tough, strong and hard Corrosion resistant | Medical instruments |
| Non-ferrous | d) | Excellent conductor | Electrical wiring |
| Non-ferrous alloy | Brass | e) | f) |

[6

# Materials: Polymers

**7** Complete the table, naming one thermosetting polymer and two thermoplastic polymers. For each, give a typical application.

| | Name | Typical Application |
|---|---|---|
| Thermosetting polymer | a) | b) |
| Thermoplastic polymer | c) | d) |
| Thermoplastic polymer | e) | f) |

[6]

**8** Explain the difference between a thermoforming polymer and a thermosetting polymer.

[4]

## Materials: Textiles

**9** Using notes and/or sketches, explain the differences between knitted and woven fabrics.

[4]

**10** **10.1)** Describe the structure and properties of graphene.

[4]

**10.2)** State three potential applications of graphene.

1.

2.

3.

[3]

## Materials: New Materials

**11**  **11.1)**  Explain what is meant by a nanomaterial.

.......................................................................................................................................................

.......................................................................................................................................................  [1]

**11.2)**  Give a typical application for a nanomaterial. Explain why it is suitable for that task.

.......................................................................................................................................................

.......................................................................................................................................................

.......................................................................................................................................................

.......................................................................................................................................................  [2]

## Standard Components

**12**  **12.1)**  Name two standard components that are used with polymer products.

1. .................................................................................................................................................

2. .................................................................................................................................................  [2]

**12.2)**  Name two standard components that are used in electrical or electronic circuits.

1. .................................................................................................................................................

2. .................................................................................................................................................  [2]

**12.3)**  Name two mechanical components that are available as standard parts.

1. .................................................................................................................................................

2. .................................................................................................................................................  [2]

## Finishing Materials

13 Name **two** finishing techniques for each of the following.

Paper and board

1. ......................................................................................................................................................

2. ...................................................................................................................................................... [2]

Timber-based materials

1. ......................................................................................................................................................

2. ...................................................................................................................................................... [2]

Metal-based materials

1. ......................................................................................................................................................

2. ...................................................................................................................................................... [2]

14 What is the main purpose of finishing?

................................................................................................................................................................

................................................................................................................................................................ [1]

## Selection of Materials

15 Choose one of the following products by circling your selection.

| | | |
|---|---|---|
| Promotional flyer | Wooden toy for small children | Cooking pan |
| Plastic garden chair | Football shirt | Car gearbox |

Explain **two** important properties required by the product you have selected.

................................................................................................................................................................

................................................................................................................................................................

................................................................................................................................................................

................................................................................................................................................................ [4]

## Working with Materials

16  Describe three methods of reinforcement that can be used to increase the stiffness of a product.

Method 1 ..................................................................................................................................................

..............................................................................................................................................................

..............................................................................................................................................................

..............................................................................................................................................................

Method 2 ..................................................................................................................................................

..............................................................................................................................................................

..............................................................................................................................................................

..............................................................................................................................................................

Method 3 ..................................................................................................................................................

..............................................................................................................................................................

..............................................................................................................................................................

.................................................................................................................................... [6]

> **Total Marks** ............... / 75

# Scales of Manufacture

Quick Recall Quiz

**You must be able to:**

- Describe the characteristics and give examples of different scales of manufacture
- Explain why the equipment used changes with the scale of manufacture.

## Scales of Manufacture

- Scale of manufacture is about the number of identical products to be made.
- As the quantity of products to be made increases, the type of process that needs to be carried out, such as removing or joining material, may be the same; however, the tools and equipment used to carry out these processes may be different.

> **Key Point**
>
> The quantity of products to be made has a significant effect on the equipment selected to manufacture the products.

| Type | Characteristics | Example |
|------|-----------------|---------|
| One-off/ bespoke production | One product is made at a time.<br>This could be a prototype or an object made for a specific customer.<br>Tools and equipment are used to make many different products.<br>It usually takes a long time for each product and a high level of worker skill.<br>The cost of each product is high. | A tailored suit for a customer<br>Satellites |
| Batch production | A group of identical products are made together.<br>Once completed, another group of similar (but not necessarily identical) products may be made using the same equipment.<br>Some processes may be automated. Dedicated jigs might be used.<br>The cost of equipment to set up is typically high, so many products have to be made to bring down the cost per item made. | Furniture: tables, chairs<br>Clothing from a high street store |
| Mass production | Large quantities of identical products are needed.<br>The product typically goes through different processes on a production line.<br>The equipment is only used to make the same products, again and again. Most processes are automated with dedicated jigs and fixtures.<br>The cost per product is lower than batch manufacturing. | Cars<br>Nuts and bolts |
| Continuous production | Typically used to manufacture materials or chemicals; often these are referred to as 'commodities', as they are subsequently used in the making of other products.<br>Very large quantities of an identical material or chemical are produced, using a production line. This often runs 24 hours a day, 7 days a week.<br>The equipment is only used to make the same products, again and again. The processes are typically fully automated with dedicated jigs and fixtures.<br>The initial set-up cost is very high. However, the cost per product made is low compared to other methods. | Petrol<br>Steel |

# Influence of Quantity on Selection of Equipment

- As the quantity of products to be made increases there are increasing opportunities for **economies of scale**. This might involve getting discounts for buying materials in larger quantities, or reducing labour costs by moving from hand tools to automatic machines.
- For example, if someone cuts one shape from card, they may use scissors. However, if 1000 of the same shape must be cut, a laser cutter or a die cutter might be used: the equipment costs more but as it cuts faster and the labour time needed is reduced, so less money is needed to pay workers for each product. This means that the total cost per product of materials plus equipment plus labour can be less.

## Material Management

- Profitable manufacturing is not just about the choice of process and the level of automation: the material being processed must also be used efficiently.
- Most materials are available in a wide variety of standard shapes and sizes, called **stock forms**.
- Designers normally try to use either a stock form of material or the closest size and shape available, to minimise the amount of machining needed.
- To eliminate waste from cutting, repeating designs may be tessellated or shapes may be nested together. Digital lay planning is the use of computer software to arrange a pattern on a material.
- Some additional material may be needed for joint overlap or to allow for seams in textile products.

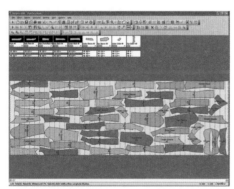
Digital lay planning

A robot arm packaging products

> ### Key Point
>
> If a large quantity of a product is being made, the total cost per product might be reduced by using automated equipment if less labour time is needed per product.

> ### Key Words
>
> one-off/bespoke
>   production
> batch production
> mass production
> continuous production
> economies of scale
> stock forms

---

### Quick Test

1. Explain what is meant by batch production.
2. Give two examples of products that are mass produced.
3. State what is meant by 'stock forms'.

# Manufacturing Processes 1: Process Types and Processes used with Paper and Board

**You must be able to:**

- Describe what is meant by wasting, addition, and deforming and reforming
- Identify the processes and equipment used to manufacture products from paper and board
- Select an appropriate tool to carry out a process needed on paper and board and justify your choice.

## Types of Manufacturing Process

- Wastage, or **wasting**, is the removal of unwanted material when making a product. For example, this could mean cutting away material, such as trimming around a pattern.
- Addition processes involve adding material to a product. This may involve joining materials together, adding layers by laminating or depositing additional materials on to the surface, for example by printing.
- Deforming and reforming processes involve changing the shape of a material without the gain or loss of material.

## Wasting Processes Used with Paper and Boards

- Tools used for cutting paper and card include:
  - scissors, which can also be used to score card
  - scalpels or craft knives, which are normally used with a safety ruler and a baseboard
  - compass cutters and circle cutters are used to cut circles in thin card
  - rotary trimmers and guillotines are used to make straight cuts in paper and card.
- A **perforation** cutter makes a row of small holes in paper or card so that a part can be torn off easily.
- **Die cutters** are used to cut shapes and holes when large numbers of products are needed. The die cutting process uses metal blades which can cut a complete net in a single operation. Creases and folds can be marked using a blunt blade. Foam rubber is often used around the blade – this compresses during cutting and pushes to release the cut material.

## Addition Processes Used with Paper and Boards

- One of the simplest methods to permanently join paper and board is by bonding using **adhesives**, such as:
  - polyvinyl acetate (PVA), either as liquid or in glue sticks
  - aerosol adhesive, also called spray mount
  - glue guns, which use heated polymers.

### Key Point

Wasting involves taking away material, addition processes involve adding material and deforming and reforming involve changing the shape.

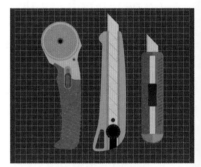
Rotary cutter and craft knives

Rotary trimmer

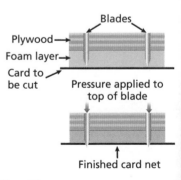

Blades
Plywood
Foam layer
Card to be cut
Pressure applied to top of blade

Finished card net

Die cutting

- **Laminating** paper involves adding layers of material, which makes a composite; for example, using heat to enclose the paper or card between two layers of plastic. Takeaway food containers can also be laminated products, made from card with layers of aluminium foil and clear polymer.
- Printing can be used to apply designs on paper, card and textiles.
- Screen printing uses simple stencils, which can each be used to apply a single colour. It is used to quickly produce cheap prints in small quantities, for example for banners.

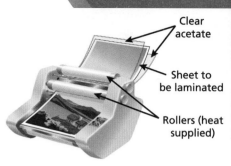

Laminating

Screen printing

| **1.** Make a screen using a wooden frame. Stretch a piece of nylon fabric (the mesh) over the frame and staple it into place. Cut out a paper stencil and place it under the screen. | **2.** Squeeze ink though the fabric mesh using a rubber strip called a 'squeegee'. | **3.** The ink will pass though the unblocked area of the stencil to produce the final printed image. |
|---|---|---|
| 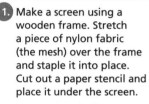 | 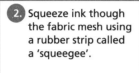 |  |

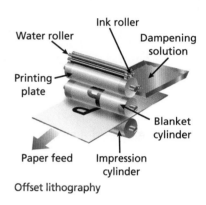

Offset lithography

- **Offset lithography** can be used to print large quantities of products, such as flyers or magazines. It works on the principle that grease and water don't mix. The image to print is in relief on the printing plate, and attracts grease (ink) applied to it. The plate is dampened, which repels ink from any non-image areas. The printing plate then transfers an inked image onto the rubber blanket cylinder, which in turn presses the image onto the paper or card as it is fed through.

# Deforming and Reforming Processes Used with Paper and Boards

- Accurate folds can be achieved in cardboard by creasing the material first, using a creasing bar. This keeps the strength of the material, whereas scoring weakens it.

**Quick Test**

1. Name six tools used to cut thin card.
2. Explain what is meant by laminating.
3. Name two printing processes.

**Key Words**

wasting
perforation
die cutting
adhesive
laminating
offset lithography

# Manufacturing Processes 2: Timber-Based Materials

**You must be able to:**

- Identify the processes and equipment used to manufacture products from timber-based materials
- Select an appropriate tool to carry out a process needed on timber-based material and justify your choice.

## Wasting Processes Typically Carried Out by Hand

- The range of sawing tools used for cutting timber-based materials includes:
  - tenon saws: used for straight cuts
  - coping saws, powered fretsaws and jigsaws: used for curved cuts
  - band saws: used for straight and curved cuts
  - circular saws: used for straight cuts in large pieces of wood.
- Chisels need a sharp edge to slice across the grain of the wood. There are four types of chisel:
  - a bevel-edged chisel is used for corners that are less than 90°
  - a firmer chisel is for general use
  - a mortise chisel is used to create deep holes for joints, such as a mortise and tenon
  - a gouge has a curved blade for carving.
- Basic chiselling actions include:
  - horizontal paring, cleaning out unwanted material by cutting across a joint
  - vertical paring, shaping the end of a piece of wood by pushing down onto the waste surface
  - chopping, digging out waste from a groove or mortise.
- Planing uses a wedge-shaped cutting blade to shave off thin layers of wood. There are several types of plane that are used by hand:
  - a jack plane is used to reduce the timber to a required size
  - a smoothing plane is used by hand to smooth the surface of the timber, before using abrasives
  - a block plane is used to plane end grain
  - a rasp or surform can be used to remove large amounts of wood when sculpting or carving shapes.
- The surface of a timber-based product can be smoothed by sanding. This uses an abrasive paper to wear away any uneven features. Sanding can be carried out by hand, using sandpaper wrapped round a sanding block, or using machines such as a belt, disc or bobbin sander.

Tenon saw

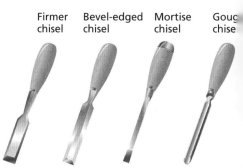

Firmer chisel    Bevel-edged chisel    Mortise chisel    Goug chise

Types of chisel

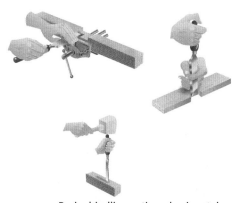

Basic chiselling actions: horizontal, vertical, chopping

Powered Planing Machine          Smoothing Pl

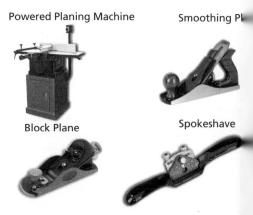

Block Plane          Spokeshave

Types of plane

# Wasting Processes Typically Carried Out Using Machines

- Thin sheets of manufactured board can be cut on a laser cutter.
- Parts with a circular profile can be made by **turning** on a wood lathe. The tool is rested on a support and moved by hand.
- Drilling makes holes by rotating a drill or boring bit clockwise as it is pushed into the material. Types of drill include portable power drills and pedestal drills (also known as pillar drills), which can be bench or floor mounted. It is important that the material is held firmly in place when drilling.
- A planer-thicknesser machine uses a rotary cutter to plane large pieces of timber to a required size.
- Computer numerical control (**CNC**) routers are used to make grooves and edge profiles. They use computer-controlled stepper motors to move the router and are very common in the furniture industry and school workshops.

Turning

## Addition Processes

- Timber parts can be permanently bonded together using polyvinyl acetate (PVA) adhesive.
- Laminating can also be used to make curved wooden shapes, such as chair seats. Adhesive is applied to the surfaces of many thin layers of wood. These are then clamped into a mould or **former** of the shape required. Once the adhesive has set, the layers of wood become a single product in the shape of the mould.

Headstock

'Outside' spindle with left hand thread

'Inside' spindle with right hand thread

Dead centre

Tool rest

'Tee' tool rest

Tailstock

Swivel arm

Wood-turning lathe

## Deforming and Reforming

- Strips of timber can be bent by heating them in steam until they become pliable. They can then be shaped round a former. The wood must be clamped in place until it is cool.
- Thin sheets (plies) of timber can be glued together and shaped around a former. They must be clamped in place until they dry. This is called laminating.

> **Key Point**
>
> There is a wide variety of different wasting tools; most are designed to carry out specific tasks.

### Quick Test

1. Name four types of saw used to cut wood.
2. Name an adhesive used to permanently bond together wooden parts.
3. State two ways of making a curved shape from flat timber.

> **Key Words**
>
> turning
> CNC
> former

# Manufacturing Processes 3: Metals and Alloys

Quick Recall Quiz

**You must be able to:**

- Identify the processes and equipment used to manufacture products from metal and alloys
- Select an appropriate tool to carry out a process needed on a metal or alloy and justify your choice.

## Wasting Processes

- Metal can be sawn by hand using a hacksaw or, for small pieces, a junior hacksaw. Thin sheet can be cut on a band saw and thicker pieces can be cut using a powered hacksaw.
- Drilling can be used to make holes, using portable power drills and pedestal drills.
- **Shearing** is used to cut thin metal sheet, using metal shears (also known as tin snips) or a guillotine. The force applied along the cutting edge literally pushes the metal apart.
- Circular profiles can be made by turning metal using a centre lathe. The work piece is normally held in a chuck and rotated against a blade. The cutting tool can be moved left and right, in or out. Lathes can also be used to cut internal or external threads.
- Milling uses a rotating tool to make flats or grooves in metal. The position of the tool on the work piece can be controlled either manually or using computer-controlled stepper motors.

Metal shears

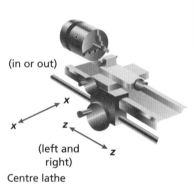

(in or out)

(left and right)

Centre lathe

## Addition Processes

- Metals can be joined together or to other materials using an epoxy resin type of adhesive. However, the joint is typically much weaker than the metal.
- **Welding** uses heat to melt the edges of the metals being joined, normally with extra added 'filler' metal. When the melted metals cool they form the joint. The heat can be from a flame or an electric arc.
- **Brazing** is carried out at a lower temperature than welding. Unlike welding, the parts being joined are not melted. An added filler metal is melted and flows between the parts to form the joint.

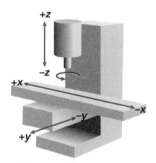

Milling machine

## Deforming Processes

- Bars and pipes can be bent round a former. A bar might be heated to make it easier to bend.
- Metal plates can be bent and curved by feeding them between rollers moving at different speeds. The more times this is repeated, the smaller the radius of the curve.
- Sheet metal can be folded using a press which forces the metal against an angled former to bend it.

Welding a steel pipe

 **Key Point**

Deforming uses large forces to permanently change the metal's shape.

- **Presses** are also used to bend and form sheet metal and stamp out holes. The presses use massive pressure from hydraulic rams, to make products such as car body panels.

Metal plate bending machine

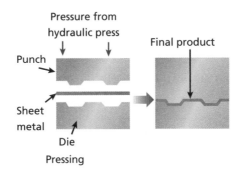
Pressing

Metal folding

## Reforming Processes

- **Casting** can be used to make 3D products from metal. It involves pouring molten metal into a mould where it cools. Any waste material can be re-melted and used again.
- Sand casting is used to cast aluminium and cast iron.
  - The mould is made using a pattern. This is sandwiched between two boxes of sand, called a cope and drag.
  - Once sand is compressed around the pattern, the cope and drag are carefully separated and the pattern removed, leaving a hollow shape.
  - There will also be holes for a runner, to allow the metal to be poured in, and a riser, to let air escape.
  - When the cope and drag are put back together the liquid metal can be poured in.
- Unlike sand casting, **die casting** uses a reusable metal mould. Molten metal is poured into a cylinder. A ram then forces this metal into the mould, holding pressure until it has cooled. The mould is then opened and the component removed. Due to the cost of the mould, die casting is typically only used when large quantities of products are to be made.

Casting molten aluminium into moulds

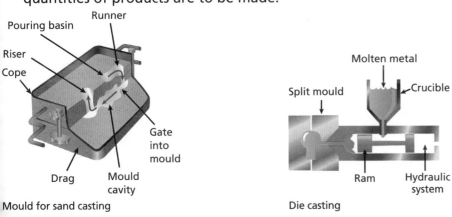
Mould for sand casting

Die casting

### Quick Test

1. What machine is used to turn metal parts with a circular profile?
2. List three ways of permanently joining two pieces of metal.
3. What is the purpose of a riser in a mould for sand casting?

# Manufacturing Processes 4: Polymers

**You must be able to:**

- Identify the processes and equipment used to manufacture products from polymers
- Select an appropriate tool to carry out a process needed on a polymer and justify your choice.

## Wasting Processes

- Thin sheet polymers can be sawn using coping saws, powered fretsaws and band saws.
- Similar to timber and metals, holes can be drilled using portable power drills and pedestal drills.

## Addition Processes

- Solvent cement is a type of adhesive that only creates bonds in polymers. It dissolves the surface of the polymer parts, so that they can mix together and form a joint as they solidify.
- Thermoplastic parts can be welded together. The faces to be joined can be heated using an electrically heated welding gun or a hot plate. On melting they are pushed together, forming the joint as they cool.
- 3D printing involves printing out a product directly from a CAD model. It enables a complex product to be made in a single operation, where several complex machines may have been needed previously. The CAD model is split into multiple layers by a computer, and the 3D printer deposits material one layer at a time, building up the finished item.

## Deforming and Reforming Processes

- Simple bends can be made in thermoplastics using a line bender. This heats just the area where the bend is needed until it is flexible. The plastic can then be held against a former or jig until it cools.
- Three-dimensional products can be made using moulding processes. For example:
  - Press or yoke moulding: plastic sheet is heated in an oven until it is flexible. It is then pressed between a mould and a yoke (also know as a male and female mould, respectively). Once cooled, it retains the shape of the mould.
  - In vacuum forming, the pressure pushing the heated plastic onto the mould comes from the atmosphere, when the air between the mould and plastic is sucked out.
- Injection moulding is a type of casting process that can be used to make complex 3D shapes. Plastic powder or granules are fed from a hopper into the machine. Heaters melt the plastic as the screw

Bench-top pedestal drill

3D printing

### Key Point

Most industrial polymer moulding processes use reusable metal moulds and are designed to make products in quantity.

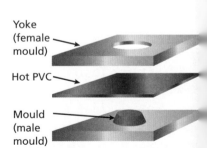

Yoke (female mould)

Hot PVC

Mould (male mould)

Yoke moulding

moves it along towards the mould. Once enough plastic has been melted, the screw forces the plastic into the mould. Pressure is maintained on the mould, until it has cooled enough to be opened.

- **Extrusion** is similar to injection moulding, but does not use a mould. The plastic is forced through a die in a continuous stream, creating long tubes or sections.
- **Blow moulding** is similar to extrusion, but an air supply and a split mould are used. It is used to make hollow products, such as drinks bottles.

Vacuum-forming process

| 1. The plastic is heated and the mould moves close to it. Air is 'sucked out' to form a vacuum. | 2. This causes the hot plastic to be sucked onto the mould. As the temperature of the plastic falls, a rigid impression of the mould is formed. | 3. The vacuum pump is turned off, allowing air to enter. The former is lowered, separating it from the final product. |
|---|---|---|
| 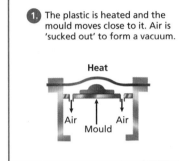 | 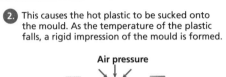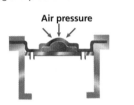 | 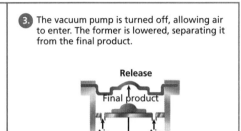 |

Injection moulding

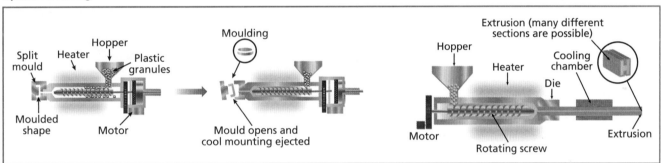

Blow moulding

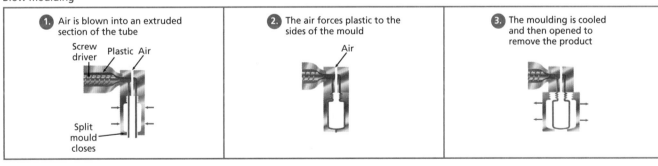

| 1. Air is blown into an extruded section of the tube | 2. The air forces plastic to the sides of the mould | 3. The moulding is cooled and then opened to remove the product |
|---|---|---|

### Key Words

line bending
moulding
vacuum forming
injection moulding
extrusion
blow moulding

### Quick Test

1. Name three types of saw used to cut polymers.
2. Describe how two polymer parts are welded together.
3. Explain the difference between injection moulding and blow moulding.

# Manufacturing Processes 5: Textiles and Electronic Systems

**You must be able to:**

- Identify the processes and equipment used to manufacture products from textiles
- Identify the processes and equipment used to manufacture electronic systems.

## Wasting Processes Used with Textiles

- Fabrics can be cut using a rotary cutter or sheared using scissors. Some can also be cut on a laser cutter.
- Pinking shears are a special type of scissor with a serrated edge, to prevent the fabric fraying.
- When large quantities of materials need to be cut, band saws can be used to quickly cut a pattern into a stack of material.

Pinking shears

## Addition Processes Used with Textiles

- **Sewing** with thread is the most common method of joining fabrics.
- Domestic sewing machines are designed to carry out a wide range of tasks. In contrast, industrial sewing machines are often designed to perform a specific type of stitch or carry out a specific task, such as making buttonholes or attaching buttons.
- An overlocker is a specialised sewing machine used to give seams and hems a professional finish or add decorative edgings.
- **Bonding** uses a strip of adhesive web placed between the fabrics to be joined. Heat from an iron then fuses them together.
- As well as bonding, adhesives can be used to laminate fabrics.
- **Quilting** creates surface texture by sandwiching wadding or stuffing between layers of fabric and stitching through the layers.
- **Piping** is a type of trim made from a strip of folded fabric inserted in a seam. It is used to define edges or style lines.

An overlocker

> ### Key Point
>
> The manufacturing techniques used will have a major influence on the shape, texture and style of a garment.

## Printing and Dyeing Textiles

- Batik is a process used to dye a pattern in cloth. Wax is applied to the surface of the cloth, either by drawing the design with a spouted tool called a canting or by printing with a copper stamp called a cap. The cloth is then soaked in a dye. Areas with the applied wax resist the dye and remain uncoloured. The wax can then be removed with boiling water. A single colour is applied each time, and the process can be repeated if multiple colours are required.

Drawing wax onto cloth

- Flatbed and rotary screen printing apply colour to fabric that moves through the machine on a conveyor belt. In flat-bed printing, an automated squeegee applies ink through a screen as the fabric progresses in a series of small movements, stopping and starting periodically. In rotary screen printing, the ink is applied by a series of rollers, and the fabric moves continuously.

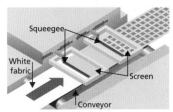

Flat-bed screen printing

## Forming Shapes in Textiles

- Shape can be added to textile garments by pressing and adding creases with an iron.
- **Gathering** allows a garment to increase fullness or widen out. It uses a sewing technique to allow a longer piece of fabric to be attached within the length of a shorter piece.
- **Pleating** is a type of gathering in which the folds are larger. It usually involves making a double or multiple fold in a textile product, held by stitching at the top or side.

Pleated skirt

## Manufacturing Electronic Systems

- Most circuits are made on printed circuit boards (PCBs). PCBs are typically made from glass epoxy, with a thin layer of copper foil laminated on one or both sides. The circuit pattern may be created by silk screen printing (using etch-resist inks), photoengraving or milling. Where needed, holes can be drilled for component legs using tungsten carbide drill bits.
- Components are typically joined to the circuit board by **soldering**. This involves melting solder to form the joint between the component and the circuit board.
- Manual soldering uses a soldering iron to melt the solder. The components are pushed through holes in the circuit board and soldered on the side with the copper tracks.
- Reflow soldering (also known as flow soldering) is used to attach surface-mounted electrical components to circuit boards. Solder paste is applied and the components positioned on their contact pads; the whole assembly is then heated to melt the solder, creating the joint.
- When making products in large quantities, pick-and-place machines are used to position surface-mounted components on the circuit board.

### Key Point

The method of making a PCB and attaching the components depends upon the quantity of circuits needed.

Manual soldering

### Key Words

sewing
bonding
quilting
piping
gathering
pleating
soldering

### Quick Test

1. Describe how two pieces of fabric can be bonded together.
2. Describe how to put a pleat in a garment.
3. Name two types of soldering process used to attach electronic components to a circuit board.

# Measurement and Production Aids

**You must be able to:**

- Explain the meaning and importance of reference points used in measurement
- Explain the reasons why production aids are used
- Describe how jigs, templates and patterns are used in product manufacture.

## Measurement and Reference Points

- Measurements are taken from a **datum surface**, or reference point on a material, product or other object.
- Sometimes two datum surfaces, at right angles to each other, are required to successfully complete a measuring task.
- Often a datum surface will need to be created on the material. For example, a hand file may be used to create a smooth surface on a piece of metal or plastic.

## The Importance of Production Aids

- To achieve accuracy and precision of production, supporting tools, known as production aids, are often required.
- The main production aids used in Design and Technology applications are **jigs**, **templates** and **patterns**.
- Jigs, templates and patterns are often used when batch producing products.
- The increase in the use of computer-aided manufacture (CAM) and computer numerical control (CNC) equipment means that jigs, templates and patterns are not as widely used as they once were, but they are still important aids when manufacturing by hand.

## Jigs

- Jigs are custom-made tools designed to achieve accuracy, repeatability and interchangeability during product manufacture.
- They are used to ensure that parts of a product are always made exactly the same, without the need for marking out.
- For example, ensuring that holes are drilled in exactly the same place on different pieces of wood.
- Printed circuit board (PCB) jigs can be used to test for faults in an electronic circuit.

> **Key Point**
>
> Production aids are required to achieve accuracy and precision of product manufacture.

The increased use of CNC equipment has reduced the need for jigs and templates, but they are still important

# Templates

- Templates are used to draw a shape onto material which can then be cut around.
- They are particularly useful when a large number of complex identical shapes have to be cut.
- They are often made from inexpensive material, such as cardboard or thin MDF.

# Patterns

- There are two types of pattern commonly used in Design and Technology applications, depending on the materials or specialism being used.
- Textiles or fabric patterns
  - These patterns are types of template that are widely used in the textiles industry.
  - They are used to trace the parts of a garment onto fabric before it is cut.
  - They are usually made from paper, but can be made from sturdier materials such as cardboard if they are to be used repeatedly.
  - Clothing manufacturers usually employ specialist pattern makers as it is a highly skilled job.
- Casting patterns
  - A different type of pattern is one which is used when casting in metal or plastic resin.
  - In this context, a pattern is used to prepare the cavity into which the molten material will be poured.
  - It is produced as a replica of the product that is to be cast. It can be made from wood, plastics or other materials.

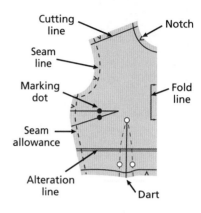

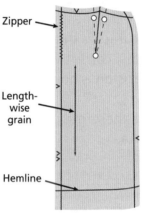

An example of a pattern used in clothing manufacture

## Key Point

Textiles or fabric patterns are used to trace the parts of a garment onto fabric before it is cut.

## Key Words

datum surface
jig
template
pattern

## Quick Test

1. What is a datum surface?
2. What is the purpose of production aids?
3. What is the main purpose of a jig?
4. What are the two types of pattern used in Design and Technology applications?

# Ensuring Accuracy

Quick Recall Quiz

**You must be able to:**

- Explain the reasons why accuracy is important when manufacturing products and prototypes
- Explain the meaning and importance of quality control and quality assurance
- Explain the importance of tolerances when manufacturing products.

## The Difference Between Accuracy and Precision

- Although the terms accuracy and precision are often used interchangeably, they actually have different meanings.
- **Accuracy** is the degree of closeness of a measurement to its true value, correct value or standard.
- **Precision** is how repeatable or reproducible the measurement is.
- It is therefore possible to be accurate but not precise, and vice versa.

## Why Accuracy is Important

- Accuracy is extremely important when manufacturing products and prototypes.
- The design specification and related drawings will give the measurements and dimensions required for the product. Just a small deviation from these can result in a product that is not fit for purpose.
- For example, if a product has two parts that must be fitted together and the distance between the holes for fasteners is wrong, it would need to be remade. This would take extra time, meaning deadlines might not be met. It would also cost extra money in terms of labour and materials.

## Tools that Improve Accuracy

- There are a wide range of tools that can be used to ensure accuracy.
- Jigs, templates and patterns are often used when batch manufacturing products. More information on the use of these tools is given on pages 104 and 105 of this revision guide.
- The increase in the use of computer-aided design (CAD)/ computer-aided manufacture (CAM) equipment has also contributed to more accurate and precise products being manufactured.

> **Key Point**
>
> It is possible to be accurate but imprecise, and vice versa.

The increased use of CAD/CAM has improved accuracy of design and manufacture

# Tolerance

- **Tolerance** is the permissible limits of variation in the dimensions or physical properties of a manufactured product or part.
- Tolerance information is usually given on drawings or product specifications.
- Manufacturers need tolerance information so that they understand the importance of the dimensions or measurements that they have been given.
- Failure to consider tolerances can lead to improper fits, wasted materials and the additional cost of remaking a product or part.
- One other specialist example is resistor tolerance:
  - this is the percentage error of a resistor's value in ohms
  - it is indicated by a gold or silver band on the resistor
  - a gold band means the resistor has a tolerance of 5%; a silver band means a tolerance of 10%; no band means a tolerance of 20%.

A resistor with a gold (5%) tolerance band

> **Key Point**
>
> Taking tolerances into account reduces the likelihood of improper fits of manufactured parts.

# Quality Control and Quality Assurance

- Although **quality control** and **quality assurance** are both about ensuring that quality products are made, they are different.
- Quality control is product-oriented whereas quality assurance is process-oriented.
- Quality control is about testing and checking that a product meets the specification or a set of defined quality standards.
- Quality assurance is about putting systems in place that ensure the quality of the processes used to manufacture the product.

> **Quick Test**
>
> 1. What is the difference between accuracy and precision?
> 2. Why is accuracy important during manufacture?
> 3. What is tolerance?
> 4. What is the main difference between quality control and quality assurance?

> **Key Words**
>
> accuracy
> precision
> tolerance
> quality control
> quality assurance

# Review Questions

## Properties of Materials

**1** Name the material property described by each of the following statements.

**1.1)** The ability of a material to resist wear or being scratched.

.......................................................................................................................................... [1]

**1.2)** The ability to conduct heat through a material.

.......................................................................................................................................... [1]

## Materials: Paper and Board

**2** Complete the table, filling in the characteristics and typical uses of different types of paper and board. The first line has been completed as an example.

| Type | Characteristics | Typical Use |
|---|---|---|
| Cartridge paper | Tough and lightly textured<br>Typically a light cream colour | Drawing |
| Layout and tracing paper | [2] | [1] |
| Solid white board | [2] | [1] |
| Corrugated cardboard | [2] | [1] |

| Foil-lined board | [2] | [1] |
| --- | --- | --- |

## Materials: Timber

**3** Explain the differences between hardwood and softwood.

[4]

**4** Using notes and/or sketches, describe the processes involved in making plywood from its raw materials into a finished board.

[4]

# Review Questions

## Materials: Metal

**5** **5.1)** State what is meant by the term 'alloy'.

...................................................................................................................................................... [1]

**5.2)** **i)** Name a ferrous metal alloy.

...................................................................................................................................................... [1]

**ii)** Give a typical use for this alloy.

......................................................................................................................................................

...................................................................................................................................................... [1]

**iii)** Explain why this alloy is an appropriate choice for this application.

......................................................................................................................................................

......................................................................................................................................................

......................................................................................................................................................

...................................................................................................................................................... [2]

**5.3)** **i)** Name a non-ferrous metal alloy.

...................................................................................................................................................... [1]

**ii)** Give a typical use for this alloy.

......................................................................................................................................................

...................................................................................................................................................... [1]

**iii)** Explain why this alloy is an appropriate choice for this application.

......................................................................................................................................................

......................................................................................................................................................

......................................................................................................................................................

...................................................................................................................................................... [2]

# Materials: Polymers

**6** Assess how polymers affect the environment through the life cycle of the material.

[10]

# Materials: Textiles

**7** Explain the difference between natural and synthetic fibres.

[2]

# Review Questions

**8**  The pie chart shows the market for technical textiles in a country divided into different sectors.

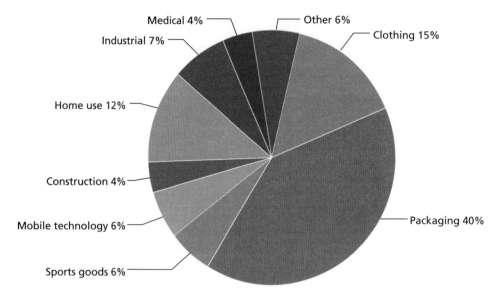

Medical 4%

Industrial 7%

Home use 12%

Construction 4%

Mobile technology 6%

Sports goods 6%

Other 6%

Clothing 15%

Packaging 40%

**8.1)** The total value of the market is £40 million.

Calculate the value of the segment for home use.

........................................................................................................................

........................................................................................................................

........................................................................................................................

........................................................................................................................ [2]

**8.2)** Calculate the fraction of the total market value that is for clothing.

Give your answer as a fraction in its lowest form.

........................................................................................................................

........................................................................................................................

........................................................................................................................

........................................................................................................................ [1]

# New Materials and Standard Components

**9** Explain what is meant by a composite material.

_____

_____

_____ [2]

**10** A manufacturer is using the following material and standard parts to manufacture a product.

| Material or component | Quantity | Cost |
|---|---|---|
| Polymer | 0.4 kg | £3 per kg |
| Screw | 8 | £0.02 each |
| Hinge | 2 | £0.32 each |

**10.1** Calculate the total material cost of the product.

_____

_____

_____

_____

_____ [3]

**10.2** The total labour cost involved in making each product is £2.48. Other costs involved in making the product (such as overheads and packaging) come to £1.72 per product. If the manufacturer wants to make a profit of 20%, what should the selling price of the product be?

_____

_____

_____

_____

_____ [3]

# Review Questions

## Finishing Materials

**11** Name **two** finishing techniques for each of the following.

Polymers

**1.** ...........................................................................................................................................

**2.** ........................................................................................................................................... [2]

Textile-based materials

**1.** ...........................................................................................................................................

**2.** ........................................................................................................................................... [2]

Electronic and mechanical systems

**1.** ...........................................................................................................................................

**2.** ........................................................................................................................................... [2]

## Selection of Materials

**12** Other than the properties of the material, state **six** factors that may be taken into consideration when selecting the material to be used in a product.

**1.** ...........................................................................................................................................

**2.** ...........................................................................................................................................

**3.** ...........................................................................................................................................

**4.** ...........................................................................................................................................

**5.** ...........................................................................................................................................

**6.** ........................................................................................................................................... [6]

**13** Choose one type of material by circling your selection.

| Paper and board | Timber | Metal alloys |
| Polymers | Textiles | Board for PCBs |

Explain **one** way in which the properties of this material type can be modified to make it more suitable for use in a product.

........................................................................................................................................

........................................................................................................................................

........................................................................................................................................ [2]

# Working with Materials

**14** State **three** ways of increasing the stiffness of a product.

1. ........................................................................................................................................

........................................................................................................................................

2. ........................................................................................................................................

........................................................................................................................................

3. ........................................................................................................................................

........................................................................................................................................ [3]

**Total Marks** ............... / 71

## Scales of Manufacture, and Manufacturing Processes 1 and 2

1. Give **two** examples of products that are typically made using each of the following scales of manufacture.

| | |
|---|---|
| One-off production | Example 1 |
| | Example 2 |
| Batch production | Example 1 |
| | Example 2 |
| Mass production | Example 1 |
| | Example 2 |
| Continuous production | Example 1 |
| | Example 2 |

[8]

**2** Describe how die cutters are used to make products from card.

................................................................................................................................................................

................................................................................................................................................................

................................................................................................................................................................

................................................................................................................................................................

................................................................................................................................................................ [3]

**3** Complete the table below, identifying the typical uses of the following tools with timber-based materials.

| Tool | Typical Tasks |
|---|---|
| Tenon saw | a) |
| Jack plane | b) |
| Mortise chisel | c) |
| Wood lathe | d) |
| Block plane | e) |
| CNC router | f) |

[10]

**4** Name **two** processes that can be used to make a curved product from sheets of natural timber.

**1.** ................................................................................................................................................................

**2.** ................................................................................................................................................................ [2]

5  Explain the difference between horizontal paring and vertical paring when using a chisel.

.................................................................................................................................

.................................................................................................................................

.................................................................................................................................

.................................................................................................................................

.................................................................................................................................

.................................................................................................................................

.................................................................................................................................

.................................................................................................................................  [4]

## Manufacturing Processes 3: Metals and Alloys

6  Name two tools that cut a metal sheet by shearing.

**1.** ...........................................................................................................................

**2.** ...........................................................................................................................  [2]

7  Using notes and/or sketches, describe how a centre lathe is used to turn a metal part.

[3]

8  Describe how a product is made by die casting.

........................................................................................................................................

........................................................................................................................................

........................................................................................................................................

........................................................................................................................................

[4]

# Manufacturing Processes 4: Polymers

9  **9.1)**  Describe how two pieces of plastic pipe can be welded together.

........................................................................................................................................

........................................................................................................................................

........................................................................................................................................

........................................................................................................................................

........................................................................................................................................

[5]

**9.2)**  Name an adhesive which can only be used to join polymers.

........................................................................................................................................

[1]

10  Using notes and/or sketches, describe the process of press moulding polymers.

[4]

# Practice Questions

## Manufacturing Processes 5: Textiles and Electronic Systems

**11** **11.1)** State two tools that can be used to cut a fabric by hand.

1. ......................................................................................................................................................... [1]

2. ......................................................................................................................................................... [1]

**11.2)** Explain the purpose of 'gathering' when making a garment from fabric.

...............................................................................................................................................................

...............................................................................................................................................................

...............................................................................................................................................................

...............................................................................................................................................................   [2]

**11.3)** Explain what is meant by 'quilting'.

...............................................................................................................................................................

...............................................................................................................................................................

...............................................................................................................................................................

...............................................................................................................................................................   [2]

**12** Describe how an electronic component is attached to a circuit board by manual soldering.

...............................................................................................................................................................

...............................................................................................................................................................

...............................................................................................................................................................

...............................................................................................................................................................

...............................................................................................................................................................

...............................................................................................................................................................

...............................................................................................................................................................   [4]

# Measurement and Production Aids, and Ensuring Accuracy

**13** Explain how measurement and production aids can help to ensure accuracy when manufacturing products. Use examples to support your answer.

[12]

**Total Marks** _____ / 68

# Impact on Industry

**You must be able to:**

- Explain the impact of new and emerging technologies on industry and enterprise
- Discuss the potential effects of the use of new and emerging technologies on employment.

## Impact on Industry

- The use of new and emerging technologies can have an impact on the design and organisation of the workplace. This can take several forms.
    - Automation and the use of robotics:
        - **Automation** is the use of computer systems and control technology to operate equipment.
        - One example of this is the use of robots in product manufacture. This can have a very positive impact on the efficiency of manufacture.
    - The way buildings and workplaces work can be improved by new technologies. For example, self-cleaning windows keep buildings looking more aesthetically pleasing and save time and maintenance costs.
    - The increased use of computer-aided manufacture (CAM), computer numerical control (CNC) and rapid prototyping equipment means that fewer hand tools are being used in product manufacture. This allows for greater accuracy and consistency of manufacture.

## Impact on Enterprise

- Effective business innovation helps to drive enterprise. This can take many different forms.

### Crowd Funding

- **Crowd funding** is a way for people to raise awareness and money for a project or idea. The enterprise will typically have a funding 'goal' that needs to be met.
- People donate money in return for rewards.
- The internet has made crowd funding very easy to implement. Websites can be set up with online payment options for people to use. Providers of crowd-funding websites typically take a percentage of the money raised.
- Crowd funding is useful for independent people or 'start-up' businesses who might struggle to gain access to more conventional sources of funding.

> **Key Point**
>
> Automation in manufacture can help to increase the efficiency of production.

Robotic arm being used in product manufacture

The use of social media to promote products is a key part of virtual marketing and retail

### Virtual Marketing and Retail

- Virtual marketing is the use of web-based marketing techniques.
- This includes the use of website banner advertising, email marketing and social media to promote products.

### Co-operatives

- A **co-operative** is a business or organisation that is run jointly by its members.
- The members share in the benefits or profits that are made.
- A co-operative benefits from the buying power of its entire membership and its democratic structure.
- A small number of people can form a co-operative, making them easy to set up.

### Fair Trade

- Fair trade is a movement that works to help people in developing countries get a fair deal for the products that they produce (for more information on fair trade see page 17).

### Planned Obsolescence

- Planned obsolescence is a business strategy where a product is designed to be no longer useful after a set period of time. This could be in terms of function, compatibility or how fashionable it is. This often results in a new or improved product replacing it.

## Impact on Employment

- One major consideration regarding the use of new and emerging technologies is the potential effect on employment.
- Many are concerned that, for example, increased automation in the workplace will result in fewer jobs being available.
- The increase in the use of CAD/CAM has resulted in fewer jobs for skilled hand machine workers, but more jobs for people trained in the use and maintenance of CAM equipment.
- Companies need to have the capacity to retrain their staff to be able to make effective use of new and emerging technologies in the workplace. In addition, workers themselves need to be increasingly flexible and able to update their skills in response to change.
- Technological change will always result in changes to job roles, particularly in design and technology. Many important jobs didn't exist as little as 5–10 years ago, and this trend is likely to grow. For example, mobile apps did not exist prior to the development of the smartphone, let alone app designers.
- Workers in the modern design and technology workplace must be literate in the use of computer-based tools.

> **Key Point**
>
> Co-operatives are run by and for the benefit of their members.

The increased use of automation has resulted in changes to the job roles of people

> **Quick Test**
>
> 1. What is crowd funding?
> 2. What is a co-operative?
> 3. What are the potential impacts of automation on employment?

> **Key Words**
>
> automation
> crowd funding
> co-operative

# Impact on Production

Quick Recall Quiz

**You must be able to:**

- Explain the impact of CAD and CAM on production
- Explain how production techniques and systems improve manufacturing efficiency.

## CAD

- **CAD** stands for **computer-aided design**.
- It is the use of computer software to produce designs for products. The designs can be 2D drawings or 3D models.

A designer using CAD software

### Advantages of CAD

- CAD is extremely accurate, often more accurate than drawing designs by hand.
- It is easier to modify or revise an existing design.
- Storage space is reduced.
- Files can be shared around the world very quickly, or imported into presentations.
- 3D models can be rotated and viewed from different angles.
- Designs can be simulated to see how well they will function. This allows potential problems to be spotted early.
- Designs can be exported to CAM equipment for manufacture.

### Disadvantages of CAD

- Some CAD packages are expensive to buy, so there can be high initial setup costs.
- There needs to be access to appropriate ICT hardware to run the software. This usually needs to be a computer with a very good specification, which adds to the cost.
- Some designers may not be familiar with how to use CAD software, so time and money must be spent training them. They must also regularly update their skills.

## CAM

- **CAM** stands for **computer-aided manufacture**.
- It is the use of computer software to control machine tools to manufacture products.
- Examples of CAM equipment include laser cutters, vinyl cutters and 3D plotters.

### Key Point

CAD/CAM improve accuracy of design and manufacture, but often require high initial setup costs to be paid.

### Advantages of CAM

- Complex shapes can be produced much more easily than when manufacturing by hand.
- There is consistency of manufacture as every product produced is exactly the same.
- It enables very high levels of manufacturing precision and accuracy.
- There is greater efficiency as machines can run 24 hours a day, 7 days a week.
- It can increase the speed of manufacture, especially when producing products in large numbers.

---

**Disadvantages of CAM**

- As with CAD initial setup costs can be high. CAM machines are usually very expensive, although their cost is reducing with time.
- Operators must be trained to use the equipment, which adds time and cost.
- For one-off products, CAM can actually be slower than if the product was produced by hand.

# Improving Manufacturing Efficiency

- **Lean manufacturing** is an approach that aims to make products in the most effective and efficient way possible. Lean manufacturing involves eliminating all forms of waste during manufacturing. Waste here is not referring just to rubbish or removed material: it refers to any activity that does not add value to the product. For example, waste includes:
  - moving products around a factory
  - time workers spend looking for tools
  - making too many products
  - doing more to the product than the customer needs
  - making defective parts.
- Typically, most manufacturers have a stock of materials waiting to be processed. This is a waste as stock costs money, which is tied up in the company. With **just-in-time production** (JIT production), suppliers deliver materials only when they are needed. This means less money is tied up in materials. However, if suppliers don't deliver on time or there are quality problems, this can stop production, meaning that expensive equipment is standing around unused and deadlines are missed.
- Flexible manufacturing systems (FMS) can react in the event of predicted or unpredicted change. This can include the need for the system to be changed to make new products or changes to the order of operations that make a product.
- Increased automation is improving manufacturing efficiency, but can result in fewer jobs for people.

# Technology Push and Market Pull

- **Technology push** is when new products are produced because of new materials or manufacturing methods becoming available. Research and development is a key part of this process.
- **Market pull** is when new products are developed because of market forces. Market research is a common tool used by design companies to gauge the opinion of the marketplace.

A laser cutter in operation

> **Key Point**
>
> Different production systems and techniques can be used to improve manufacturing efficiency.

Automation can be used to improve manufacturing efficiency

> **Key Words**
>
> computer-aided design (CAD)
> computer-aided manufacture (CAM)
> lean manufacturing
> just-in-time production
> technology push
> market pull

---

> **Quick Test**
>
> 1. What is meant by the terms 'CAD' and 'CAM'?
> 2. What is lean manufacturing?
> 3. What is the difference between technology push and market pull?

# Impact on Society and the Environment

Quick Recall Quiz

**You must be able to:**

- Explain the impact of new and emerging technologies on sustainability and the environment
- Discuss the potential effects of new designs on culture and society.

## Impact on Sustainability and the Environment

- Resource consumption, such as the sourcing of raw materials, impacts on the future of the planet.
- Finite resources are resources that will eventually run out. For example, many products are made using timber-based products. Trees should be replanted to ensure a continuous supply and prevent deforestation.
- Non-finite resources are resources that are easy to replenish. Making greater use of these can help to improve the sustainability of products.
- Designers should aim to reduce the amount of waste that is created through designing, making and using products. This can be achieved by making products from recyclable or biodegradable materials, or making products easy to disassemble or reuse.
- New and emerging technologies can have an impact on the environment. This can be done in numerous ways:
  - **Continuous improvement** is where ongoing incremental improvements are made to a product or process.
  - Efficient working can reduce waste, in terms of both time and resources.
  - Pollution is a major contributor to global warming. New technologies can help to reduce this. For example, electric cars are starting to replace vehicles with pollution-causing petrol engines.

A tree being planted to replace one that has been cut down

> **Key Point**
>
> New technologies can be used to reduce pollution, such as electric car engines.

## Impact on Culture

- Changes in fashion and trends can be affected and influenced by new and emergent technologies.
  - Product designs are often influenced by what is 'in fashion' at the time. For example, clothing designs.
  - This can change continuously and designers need to keep on top of current trends if they are to keep on producing popular products.

> **Key Point**
>
> Trends can be started through the emergence and subsequent use of new technologies.

- New technologies can create trends. For example, Apple's use of applications, or apps, in their iPhone completely changed how people used their mobile phones. Apps came from nowhere to becoming something that users 'must have' on their phone.
- People with different faiths and beliefs should be respected when designing new products.

# Impact on Society

- Products can also have effects on wider society. These can be both positive and negative. Sometimes these effects are unexpected or unintended.
    - For example, mobile smartphones have completely changed how people communicate with each other in the last decade.
    - Although this means it is easier than ever to communicate with people in different locations, some feel a negative impact on society is that people do not talk directly with each other as much.
- Products should be developed so that they do not have a negative impact on others.
    - Disabled people have specific needs that must be catered for. For example, cash machines are positioned lower on walls so they can be accessed by people in wheelchairs.
    - The elderly also have specific needs and products can be designed to support them. For example, a mobile phone designed with large buttons and text.
    - Designers must also be careful not to offend people from different religious backgrounds. An example of where this can go wrong is the plastic UK £5 note that was introduced in 2016. This was found to contain animal fat, which was a problem for some Hindus and Sikhs, many of whom are vegetarian.

Inclusive and Exclusive Design

- **Inclusive design** is about designing products and systems that can be used by everyone. Ideally this should be without any special adaptations.
- Exclusive design is when products are designed for a particular group of people or a limited audience. For example, car seats are designed specifically for babies or very young children.

Apps on an Apple iPhone

A mobile phone designed with large buttons and text for elderly people

> **Key Words**
>
> continuous improvement
> trend
> inclusive design

## Scales of Manufacture, and Manufacturing Processes 1 and 2

**1**  **1.1)**  State what is meant by batch manufacturing.

.....................................................................................................................................................

.....................................................................................................................................................

.....................................................................................................................................................

.....................................................................................................................................................  [2]

**1.2)**  Give **three** examples of products that are made by batch manufacturing.

1.  ............................................................................................................................................

2.  ............................................................................................................................................

3.  ............................................................................................................................................  [3]

**2**  Using notes and/or sketches, describe how the offset lithography process is carried out.

[5]

**3** The picture shows a drill.

Identify **three** safety precautions that should be taken when using the drill. For each, give a reason why it is needed.

Bench drill

| Safety Precaution | Reason this is Needed |
|---|---|
| **1.** | |
| **2.** | |
| **3.** | |

[6]

**4** Describe how a curved shape is made in natural timber by steam bending.

[5]

## Manufacturing Processes 3: Metals and Alloys

**5** Name **two** methods that can be used to bend a metal sheet.

**1.** ................................................................................................................................................

**2.** ................................................................................................................................................ **[2]**

**6** Complete the table, identifying the tools or machines that would be used to carry out the task listed.

| Task | Tool or Machine Typically Used |
|---|---|
| Cutting a metal bar by hand | **a)** .................................................................... |
| Turning a circular profile on a metal bar | **b)** .................................................................... |
| Making a hole in a metal plate | **c)** .................................................................... |
| Making a flat or a groove in a metal part | **d)** .................................................................... |

**[4]**

**7** A manufacturer has an order from a customer for 10 identical cast parts.

Explain why the manufacturer might prefer to use sand casting rather than die casting for this task.

.........................................................................................................................................................

.........................................................................................................................................................

.........................................................................................................................................................

.........................................................................................................................................................

.........................................................................................................................................................

.........................................................................................................................................................

.........................................................................................................................................................

.........................................................................................................................................................

.........................................................................................................................................................

......................................................................................................................................................... **[4]**

# Manufacturing Processes 4: Polymers

**8** Name **two** types of saw that are used to cut polymer sheet.

1. ....................................................................................................................................................

2. ....................................................................................................................................................  [2]

**9** Explain how a polymer part is produced by 3D printing.

......................................................................................................................................................

......................................................................................................................................................

......................................................................................................................................................

......................................................................................................................................................

......................................................................................................................................................

......................................................................................................................................................

......................................................................................................................................................  [4]

**10** Using notes and/or sketches, describe how a plastic bottle is made by blow moulding.

[4]

# Review Questions

## Manufacturing Processes 5: Textiles and Electronic Systems

**11** State what an overlocker is used for in textiles.

[1]

**12** Describe how rotary screen printing is used in textile manufacturing.

[4]

**13** Explain the differences between manual and flow soldering.

[6]

# Measurement and Production Aids, and Ensuring Accuracy

**14** **14.1)** Define the following terms.

Jig

.......................................................................................................

.......................................................................................................

.......................................................................................................

Tolerance

.......................................................................................................

.......................................................................................................

....................................................................................................... [4]

**14.2)** Explain why it is important to use tolerances when manufacturing products.

.......................................................................................................

.......................................................................................................

.......................................................................................................

.......................................................................................................

.......................................................................................................

....................................................................................................... [3]

**Total Marks** .............. / 59

## Impact on Industry, and Impact on Society and Environment

**1**   **1.1)**   Which of the following statements best describes the term 'co-operative'? Tick the correct box.

a) A business jointly owned and run by its members. ☐

b) A method of marketing and selling a product. ☐

c) A method of raising funding and awareness for a project. ☐

d) A way of ensuring producers of products get a fair deal. ☐   [1]

**1.2)**   Explain why it is important to consider people of different cultures when designing products. Include an example in your answer.

........................................................................................................................................

........................................................................................................................................

........................................................................................................................................

........................................................................................................................................

........................................................................................................................................

........................................................................................................................................ [3]

**1.3)**   Explain **one** benefit of using continuous improvement techniques in manufacturing.

........................................................................................................................................

........................................................................................................................................

........................................................................................................................................

........................................................................................................................................ [2]

# Impact on Production

2 Give **three** advantages and **two** disadvantages of using CAD to design prototypes.

Advantage 1

............................................................................................................................................

............................................................................................................................................

Advantage 2

............................................................................................................................................

............................................................................................................................................

Advantage 3

............................................................................................................................................

............................................................................................................................................

Disadvantage 1

............................................................................................................................................

............................................................................................................................................

Disadvantage 2

............................................................................................................................................

............................................................................................................................................ [5]

**Total Marks** .................. / 11

# Review Questions

## Impact on Industry, and Impact on Society and Environment

**1** **1.1)** Give **two** advantages and **one** disadvantage of increased automation in manufacturing.

Advantage 1

......................................................................................................................................

......................................................................................................................................

Advantage 2

......................................................................................................................................

......................................................................................................................................

Disadvantage

......................................................................................................................................

...................................................................................................................................... **[3]**

**1.2)** Describe the difference between a finite and a non-finite resource.

......................................................................................................................................

......................................................................................................................................

......................................................................................................................................

...................................................................................................................................... **[2]**

# Impact on Production

**2** Give **three** advantages and **two** disadvantages of using CAM to produce prototypes.

Advantage 1

.................................................................................................................................................................................

.................................................................................................................................................................................

Advantage 2

.................................................................................................................................................................................

.................................................................................................................................................................................

Advantage 3

.................................................................................................................................................................................

.................................................................................................................................................................................

Disadvantage 1

.................................................................................................................................................................................

.................................................................................................................................................................................

Disadvantage 2

.................................................................................................................................................................................

............................................................................................................................................................... [5]

Total Marks ................... / 10

# Mixed Exam-Style Questions

**1** A manufacturer is making a plastic product using the injection moulding process.

**1.1)** Using notes and/or sketches, describe the injection moulding process.

[5]

**1.2)** The volume of plastic in one product is $2.4 \times 10^{-5}$ m³. After making 20 000 products, the manufacturer finds that he has used 0.5 m³ of material.

Calculate the volume of material that has been lost as waste during the manufacturing process.

[2]

**1.3)** The manufacturer has calculated that the total cost of each product will be £6.40.

The selling price is £8.00. Calculate the percentage profit.

[2]

2   Using notes and/or sketches, describe how a product is made using sand casting.

[10]

③ The table lists the tools and equipment used for wasting different materials.

Complete the missing information. The first row has been completed as an example.

| Material | Tool | Used for |
|---|---|---|
| Paper | Punch | Making holes |
| Wood | a) | Making straight cuts by hand |
| Thin card | Compass cutters | b) |
| c) | Metal shears | Cutting thin sheet |
| d) | Rotary trimmer | e) |
| Textiles | f) | Cutting a serrated edge to stop material fraying |
| Metal | g) | Turning round parts |

[7]

4 A design is being produced for a child's night light. The night light must:

- Automatically detect when it has become dark

- Light up for a timed period after it has gone dark.

**4.1)** Give a suitable input and output device for the night light.

Input

.....................................................................................................................................................

Output

..................................................................................................................................................... [2]

**4.2)** The designer has decided to use a microcontroller as the process of the system.

Explain **two** reasons why this would be a good choice.

**1.** ..........................................................................................................................................

.....................................................................................................................................................

.....................................................................................................................................................

.....................................................................................................................................................

**2.** ..........................................................................................................................................

.....................................................................................................................................................

.....................................................................................................................................................

..................................................................................................................................................... [4]

5  Complete the table, which lists how mechanical devices convert between types of motion. The first line has been completed as an example.

| Device | Type of Motion Input | Type of Motion Output |
|---|---|---|
| Pulley | Rotary motion | Rotary motion |
| a) | Linear motion | Linear motion in opposite direction |
| Rack and pinion | b) | c) |
| Cam | Rotary | d) |

[4]

6  A team of designers is developing an electric vehicle. To transfer the motion from the motor to the wheels they are considering using either pulleys and belts or two spur gears. Compare the advantages and disadvantages of these two approaches.

[6]

**7** **7.1)** Explain how designers can ensure that their products are sustainable.

............................................................................................................................................................

............................................................................................................................................................

............................................................................................................................................................

............................................................................................................................................................

............................................................................................................................................................

............................................................................................................................................................

............................................................................................................................................................

............................................................................................................................................................ **[4]**

**7.2)** Define the term 'product miles'.

............................................................................................................................................................

............................................................................................................................................................

............................................................................................................................................................

............................................................................................................................................................ **[2]**

**7.3)** Explain why it is important to reduce oceanic pollution.

............................................................................................................................................................

............................................................................................................................................................

............................................................................................................................................................

............................................................................................................................................................ **[2]**

**8** Identify the types of motion represented by each of the diagrams.

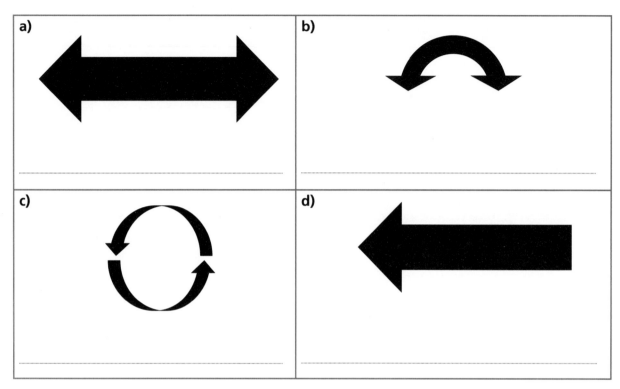

a)

b)

c)

d)

[4]

**9** The diagram shows a lever.

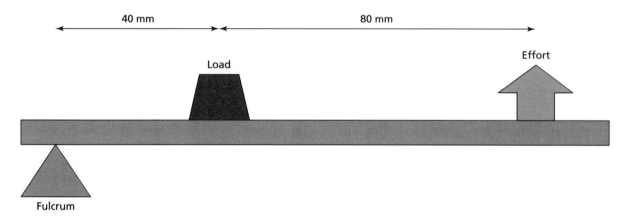

40 mm

80 mm

Effort

Load

Fulcrum

**9.1)** State the order of the lever.

[1]

**9.2)** The load is 40 mm from the fulcrum. The effort is 80 mm from the load.

Calculate the mechanical advantage.

[2]

**10** **10.1)** State what is meant by just-in-time manufacturing.

[1]

**10.2)** Why do companies use just-in-time manufacturing?

[3]

11  Using notes and/or sketches, describe how extruded tubes are made from polymer.

[5]

12  Identify **two** computer-based tools that are used in the design and communication of products. For each, explain how it is used.

Computer-based tool 1 ........................................................................................................

Explanation ......................................................................................................................

.........................................................................................................................................

......................................................................................................................................... [3]

Computer-based tool 2 ........................................................................................................

Explanation ......................................................................................................................

.........................................................................................................................................

......................................................................................................................................... [3]

**13** **13.1)** Explain **two** advantages and **one** disadvantage of just-in-time manufacturing.

Advantage 1 .................................................................................................................................

..........................................................................................................................................................

..........................................................................................................................................................

..........................................................................................................................................................

Advantage 2 .................................................................................................................................

..........................................................................................................................................................

..........................................................................................................................................................

..........................................................................................................................................................

Disadvantage .................................................................................................................................

..........................................................................................................................................................

..........................................................................................................................................................

.......................................................................................................................................................... [6]

**13.2)** Explain the purpose of lean manufacturing.

..........................................................................................................................................................

..........................................................................................................................................................

..........................................................................................................................................................

.......................................................................................................................................................... [2]

Total Marks ..................... / 80

# Answers

### Page 9 Quick Test
1. A cyclic design approach where each iteration is tested, evaluated and refined, resulting in a new iteration.
2. Greater sense of user ownership in final product; constant user feedback.
3. When designing electronic, mechanical or mechatronic systems.

### Page 11 Quick Test
1. Input, process, driver and output
2. They have a resistance that varies depending on the light level.
3. Flowcharts, block editors or raw code
4. Light: lamp; sound, buzzer or speaker

### Page 13 Quick Test
1. Norman Foster/Foster + Partners
2. Bauhaus
3. Aldo Rossi.
4. Sir Alec Issigonis

### Page 15 Quick Test
1. It combined computing/internet technology with a digital music player and a mobile phone.
2. The bagless vacuum cleaner
3. To keep athletes cool and dry
4. To eliminate harmful toxins from its clothing

### Page 17 Quick Test
1. Reduce, rethink, refuse, recycle, reuse, repair
2. Guaranteed minimum price for most products; Fairtrade Premium to spend on improving lifestyles
3. Damage to marine life and habitats

### Design Strategies and Electronic Systems
1. **1.1)** 1 mark for each correct response.

| Function | Component | Input, Process or Output |
|---|---|---|
| Detect changes in light level | LDR [1] | Input [1] |
| Produce light | Lamp [1] | Output [1] |
| Produce sound | Buzzer [1] or speaker [1] | Output [1] |
| Detect changes in temperature | Thermistor [1] | Input [1] |
| Be programmed to turn an output on for a set period of time | Microcontroller [1] | Process [1] |

**1.2)** 1 mark for definition. For example: a framework where the needs and wants of users are given attention at each stage of the design process [1].

### The Work of Others: Designers
2. 1 mark for each designer, 1 mark for each appropriate design and up to 2 marks for each explanation of influence. For example:
   - Designer: Harry Beck [1]; design: London Underground Map [1]; influence: used a layout inspired by electronic schematics [1] which has been emulated for use in many transport systems worldwide [1].
   - Designer: Norman Foster [1]; design: 30 St Mary Axe/the 'Gherkin' [1]; influence: pioneered energy-saving methods [1] which allowed it to use half the energy of similar sized buildings [1].

### The Work of Others: Companies
3. 1 mark for each company, 1 mark for each appropriate design and up to 2 marks for each explanation of influence. For example:
   - Company: Alessi [1]; design: Juicy Salif lemon squeezer [1]; influence: has a distinctive form [1], showing that everyday household objects can be designed to be interesting to look at [1].
   - Company: Apple [1]; design: iPhone [1]; influence: reinvented the concept of the mobile phone [1] by combining a phone with a digital music player and internet capability [1].

### Ecological, Environmental and Social Issues
4. For each term award 1 mark for correct definition. Reuse: using the materials/components again in another product [1]. Recycle: reprocessing the materials/components used for use in another product [1]. Refuse: deciding not to use unsustainable materials/components in a product [1]. Rethink: finding a better, more sustainable way to solve the design problem [1]. Reduce: using less material/fewer components in the product [1]. Repair: designing the product so it is easy to fix if it breaks [1].

### Page 23 Quick Test
1. A group of people assembled to discuss and give feedback on a product or a product idea.
2. Primary data is from original research, secondary data is from other sources.
3. Measurements taken from millions of people and put in charts. Used to ensure products are easy to use and interact with.

### Page 25 Quick Test
1. A short description of the design problem and how it is to be solved.
2. A set of measurable criteria for the design.
3. Details surrounding scale of production, assembly details, materials needed and quality control and quality assurance.

### Page 27 Quick Test
1. Sketching, modelling, testing, evaluation
2. To get first ideas down on paper quickly.
3. To check the effectiveness of a pattern that has been produced for a garment.
4. It uses real components, so is accurate.

### Page 29 Quick Test
1. Freehand, perspective, isometric projection
2. 30°
3. To show how the parts in an assembly fit together.

### Page 31 Quick Test
1. Plan/top, front and side
2. For example, any two of: calculating the values of components to use in an electrical circuit, designing the shape of speedboat hulls, determining how strong a bridge needs to be, simulating the testing of products.
3. Card modelling, toiles, breadboarding

### Page 33 Quick Test
1. Allows face-to-face meetings to take place from different locations, almost anywhere in the world.
2. Produces visual aids that add interest to a presentation; allows sharing of photographs and technical information of a design.
3. Bill of materials

### Page 35 Quick Test
1. A full-sized, actual version or primary example of an intended product or system.
2. So the designer can ensure that the final product meets their needs.
3. So the designer can learn how well the product being developed would meet the needs of the brief, specification and/or client.

**Design Strategies, and Ecological, Environmental and Social Issues**
1. **1.1)** Up to 2 marks for explanation of one benefit. For example: guarantees a minimum price for most products [1] so that even if global prices fall producers will still get a fair price [1].
**1.2)** Up to 2 marks for explanation. For example: it might cost more to buy [1] which would make it unappealing for people on tight budgets [1].
**1.3)** 1 mark for definition of the term. For example: the clearing of forest area into non-forest land [1].
**1.4)** Up to 2 marks for explanation. For example: a cyclic process where each iteration of a design is tested and evaluated [1]. Changes and refinements are then made, leading to a new iteration [1].

**Electronic Systems**
2. 1 mark for showing how/where the program starts and ends, 1 mark for way of checking the switch has been pressed, 1 mark for turning on the buzzer after the switch has been pressed, 1 mark for way of setting the correct time period, 1 mark for turning the buzzer off, 1 mark for turning on the lamp. Any appropriate programming language may be used, including raw code, block or flowchart-based approaches.

**The Work of Others: Designers**
3. 1 mark for each designer and up to 3 marks for each description of impact. For example:
* Designer: Mary Quant [1]; impact: was an influential figure in the popular Mod fashion movement [1]. Encouraged people to dress to please themselves [1]. Took credit for the design of the miniskirt [1].
* Designer: Gerrit Rietveld [1]; impact: part of the De Stijl design movement [1]. Designed famous red and blue chair [1]. Aimed for simplicity in construction [1].

**The Work of Others: Companies**
4. 1 mark for each company, 1 mark for each product and up to 2 marks for each description. For example:
* Company: Dyson [1]; product: bagless vacuum cleaner [1]; description; uses cyclone to separate dust [1], stores dirt in see through plastic container [1].
* Company: Under Armour [1]; product: moisture-wicking t-shirt [1]; description: made from moisture-wicking synthetic fabric [1], keeps athletes cool and dry [1].

**Research and Investigation**
1. **1.1)** Up to 2 marks. For example: measurements taken from large numbers of people [1] and put together in charts [1].
**1.2)** Up to 3 marks for explanation. For example: check charts showing head circumferences [1]. This would assist in creating appropriate sizes for the helmet design [1] so that it would properly fit a large number of firefighters [1].
**1.3)** 1 mark for each correct definition. Primary data: data that is obtained first hand [1]. Secondary data: data that is available/obtained from other parties [1].

**Briefs and Specifications**
2. 1 mark for each correct answer. **2.1)** d; **2.2)** c; **2.3)** b

**Exploring and Developing Ideas**
3. **3.1)** 1 mark for each appropriate answer. For example: Electronic circuit: breadboard [1]; wedding dress: toile [1]; early idea for a mobile phone case: card model [1].
**3.2)** 1 mark for each correct answer. For example: sketching [1], testing [1], evaluating [1].

**Communication of Ideas**
4. Award marks as follows, up to a maximum of 4 marks:
* Correctly identifying/using the vanishing point, extended from the wall edges [1].

* Vertical lines are all at 90° to the horizontal plane/horizon line [1].
* Horizontal lines in cooker extend towards the vanishing point [1].
* Cooker is correctly located half way along the right wall [1].
* Cooker is well drawn and in appropriate size [1].
5. Award 1 mark each for up to three of the following, with a second mark for each for stating its use:
* 3D CAD drawing [1], for example to show how parts in an assembly fit together [1].
* Card modelling [1] or 3D printing [1], for example to create the physical appearance of the item [1].
* Producing a toile [1] to test the design for a garment [1].
* Breadboarding [1] to test the operation of a circuit [1].

**Computer-Based Tools**
6. 1 mark for each suitable example and 1 mark each for further description.
* Produce a bill of materials to show the client [1] using spreadsheet software [1].
* Produce a visual presentation of initial design ideas [1] using presentation software [1].
* Produce a simulation of how the design works [1] using CAD software [1].

**Prototype Development**
7. **7.1)** 1 mark per suitable point or 2 marks for a point explained further. For example: shows how the product will look/function [1] so that clients can decide if they are happy or not with the design [1]. Potential problems with the design can be identified early [1] thus ensuring the final product is fit for purpose [1].
**7.2)** 1 mark per suitable point or 2 marks for a point explained further. For example: it is easy to cut to size/shape [1] so specialist cutting tools are not needed [1]. It is cheap to buy [1] so can be used in large quantities [1].

**Page 47 Quick Test**
1. They are burned to create steam. This then turns turbines, which drive the generators that produce electricity.
2. Solar, wind, hydro-electrical, tidal and biomass
3. They are clean, sustainable and will not run out.

**Page 49 Quick Test**
1. Both move back and forwards, but reciprocating motion is in a straight line whereas oscillating motion swings down and up.
2. Rigid bar, fulcrum, load and effort
3. Third-order lever

**Page 51 Quick Test**
1. Rotary to reciprocating motion
2. Spur, bevel, worm and worm wheel, rack and pinion
3. It would make the pulley wheels run in opposite directions.

**Research and Investigation**
1. 1 mark for each correct answer. **1.1)** d; **1.2)** c; **1.3)** a

**Briefs and Specifications**
2. Up to 2 marks for each definition. Design brief: a short description of the design problem [1] and how it is to be solved [1]. Design specification: a set of measurable design targets [1] that the product must meet [1]. Manufacturing specification: a set of information about how the product is to be manufactured [1] such as scale of production [1].

**Exploring and Developing Ideas**
3. 7–9 marks: thorough knowledge and understanding of the steps taken when developing design ideas using an iterative

# Answers

process. All points fully explained. 4–6 marks: good knowledge and understanding of the importance of the steps taken when developing design ideas using an iterative process. Some points explained further. 1–3 marks: limited knowledge or understanding. Mainly descriptive response.

Indicative answer: iterative process: a cyclic process where each iteration is tested, evaluated and refined, leading to a new iteration. Sketching: a quick way to get initial ideas down on paper; freehand sketching does not need to follow drawing conventions. Modelling: models are made to check how a design will look and function in 3D. They can also be presented to clients and stakeholders to gain feedback. Card is a good modelling material to use as it is cheap and easy to cut. Testing and evaluating: each iteration of a design should be tested and evaluated to assess how well it does the job that it is supposed to do. The client or end user should be involved in this process. This then leads to refinements and improvements being made.

### Communication of Ideas

4. To show how the parts of a product are located in relation to each other [1]. It can be used when assembling products [1].
5. Award up to two marks as follows: 'horizontal' lines are positioned at 30° to the baseline [1]; vertical lines (such as the front edge) go straight up [1]; lines are in proportion to the size of the object [1].
6. 6.1) Third angle [1]
   6.2) i) Top/plan [1]
      ii) Front [1]
      iii) Side [1]

### Computer-Based Tools

7. 1 mark for each correct answer. 7.1) d; 7.2) a; 7.3) b

### Prototype Development

8. 7–9 marks: thorough knowledge and understanding of the considerations that designers must take account of when developing prototypes. All points fully discussed. 4–6 marks: good knowledge and understanding of the considerations that designers must take account of when developing prototypes. Some points discussed further. 1–3 marks: limited knowledge or understanding. Mainly descriptive response.

Indicative answer: does it satisfy the requirements of the brief, the specification and the client? Has the client been consulted or given feedback on the prototype? Is the prototype innovative or creative? Will it offer something original to the market? Does it function as expected? Is it fit for its intended purpose? Is it aesthetically pleasing? How does it appeal to the five senses? Is it easily marketable? Will it fill a gap in the market?

## Pages 58–59 Practice Questions

### Energy Generation and Storage

1. 1.1) 1 mark for each specific non-renewable source, such as coal, oil, gas or nuclear.
   1.2) 1 mark for each specific renewable source other than wind, such as solar, biomass or hydro-electricity.
   1.3) Up to 2 marks for explanation of advantage and 2 marks for explanation of disadvantage. For example:
      • Advantage: better for the environment than using fossil fuels [1] as it does not release harmful greenhouse gases into the atmosphere [1].
      • Disadvantage: will not generate electricity when there is no wind [1] which means it is limited for use on products that will be placed in windy areas [1].

### Mechanical Systems

2. 2.1) Movement in a straight line in one direction [1].
   2.2) Movement in a circle [1].

2.3) Movement backwards and forwards [1].
2.4) Swinging backwards and forwards [1].
3. 3.1) Anticlockwise [1]
   3.2) Gear ratio = 12 / 36 [1 mark for method] = 1 : 3 [1 mark for answer; must be a ratio, fractions not accepted]

## Pages 60–81 Revise Questions

### Page 61 Quick Test
1. Tension, compression, torsion, shear, bending
2. Density, thermal conductivity, electrical conductivity
3. Elasticity means that a material will return to its original shape, whereas ductility is the amount of permanent change in shape.

### Page 63 Quick Test
1. Bleached card
2. Grams per square metre, which indicates the thickness of paper or card.
3. Recycled paper cannot be used in products for food packaging.

### Page 65 Quick Test
1. Oak, birch, ash, mahogany, balsa
2. Pine, larch, spruce
3. MDF, plywood, chipboard

### Page 67 Quick Test
1. A mixture of two or more metals
2. Any three of: stainless steel, brass, high-speed steel
3. Hard and brittle, but becomes malleable between 100 and 150°C

### Page 69 Quick Test
1. Carbon-based fossil fuels
2. Liquid resins and powders
3. For example ropes, carpets, packaging

### Page 71 Quick Test
1. Knitted, woven, non-woven
2. Cotton, wool, silk
3. Coal and oil

### Page 73 Quick Test
1. Carbon
2. Less than 100 nanometres
3. Glass-reinforced polyester (GRP), carbon-reinforced polyester (CRP)

### Page 75 Quick Test
1. Nuts and bolts, rivets, machine screws (also accept hinges)
2. Screw
3. Gears, cams, pulleys, belts

### Page 77 Quick Test
1. To improve function or aesthetics
2. Polishing
3. A tactile effect and improved visual look of the product
4. To reduce the effects of friction, such as heat and noise

### Page 79 Quick Test
1. Functionality (mechanical and physical properties), aesthetics, cost, availability, environmental, social, cultural, ethical
2. Surface finish, texture, colour
3. Electrical conductivity (insulator), toughness

### Page 81 Quick Test
1. To increase the malleability
2. Folding, bending, laminating
3. Ribs of material, normally located on the inside of a product, which increase the stiffness

**Energy Generation and Storage**

1. 1.1) Up to 2 marks for explanation of each advantage. For example:
   - They are more sustainable [1] as less battery waste needs to be thrown away [1].
   - They can be recharged hundreds of times [1] so save on cost of buying new batteries [1].

   1.2) Up to 2 marks for explanation of an advantage and 2 marks for explanation of a disadvantage. For example:
   - Advantage: it can be better for the environment [1] as it is carbon-neutral [1].
   - Disadvantage: it involves the growing and caring for of crops [1] which makes it an expensive way of producing fuel [1].

**Mechanical Systems**

2. 2.1) 1 mark for a suitable example; for example, scissors, pliers, seesaw.
   2.2) Effort = load / mechanical advantage [1] = 24 / 3 = 8 Newtons [1]
   2.3) The effort needed for movement is greater than the load [1], because the effort is nearer the fulcrum than the load [1].

3. 3.1) Push–pull linkage [1]
   3.2) Bevel gears or worm and worm wheel [1]
   3.3) Cam [1]
   3.4) Rack and pinion [1]

**Properties of Materials**

1. 1.1) The ability to withstand a pulling force [1].
   1.2) The mass of material per unit volume [1].

**Materials: Paper and Board**

2. Award up to 6 marks as follows (information can be in either sketches or notes): trees are cut down [1] and turned into pulp [1]. Chemicals are added [1], such as chalk and dye [1], and the paper is formed using a mesh [1]. It is then wound into rolls [1] and subsequently cut to the required size [1].

**Materials: Timber**

3. 3.1).i) 1 mark for an appropriate answer, for example pine, larch, spruce [1].
   ii) 1 mark for a typical application of that softwood. For example (pine) construction work, joinery, furniture, (larch) boats and yachts, exterior cladding of buildings, interior panelling, (spruce) general construction, wooden aircraft frames.
   iii) 1 mark each for identifying a requirement of the application and justifying the choice with respect to one of the material properties (for example strength, weight, resistance to decay, aesthetics).

   3.2) i) 1 mark for an appropriate answer, for example oak, birch, ash, mahogany, balsa [1].
   ii) 1 mark for a typical application of that hardwood. For example (oak) high-quality furniture, (birch) furniture and cabinets, turned items, (ash) tool handles, sports equipment, wooden ladders, (mahogany) high-quality furniture, (balsa) modelling.
   iii) 1 mark each for identifying a requirement of the application and justifying the choice with respect to one of the material properties (for example strength, weight, ability to be worked, resistance to moisture, aesthetics).

4. 1 mark each for any two of: rough sawn planks, PSE planks, mouldings.

**Materials: Metals**

5. Award up to 4 marks as follows (information can be in either sketches or notes): metal ore is extracted by mining or quarrying [1]. The metal is refined using heat [1], chemical reactions [1] or electrolysis [1]. The metals are then usually melted [1] and either cast into products [1] or mechanically shaped [1].

6. a) Non-ferrous [1]
   b) Any suitable application [1]
   c) Stainless steel [1]
   d) Copper [1]
   e) Any one of: low friction, corrosion resistant. malleable [1]
   f) Any one of: locks, bearings, musical instruments [1]

**Materials: Polymers**

7. a) Any one of: epoxy resin, polyester resin, urea formaldehyde, melamine formaldehyde, phenol formaldehyde [1]
   b) Any typical application [1]
   c, e) Any one of: PET, HDPE, PVC, HIPS, PP, PMMA [1]
   d, f) Any typical application [1]

8. Award up to 4 marks as follows: a thermoforming polymer softens when heated [1] and can be reshaped [1], whereas the form of a thermosetting polymer does not change with temperature [1] and when heated it may start to char. In a thermosetting polymer the polymer chains are permanently interlinked with chemical bonds [1].

**Materials: Textiles**

9. Award up to 4 marks as follows (information can be in either sketches or notes).
   - Knitted fabrics are made from interlocking loops [1] whereas woven fabrics are constructed from interlaced yarns [1].
   - Knitted fabrics have greater elasticity than woven fabrics [1].
   - Woven fabrics have a grain due to the direction of the threads [1] and a selvedge (an edge that will not fray when cut) [1].
   - Any other relevant point.

10. 10.1) Award up to 4 marks as follows: it is made up of carbon atoms [1] arranged hexagonally in a flat 2D layer just one atom thick [1]. It is about 200 times stronger than steel [1], flexible [1], transparent [1] and conducts heat and electricity well [1].
    10.2) Award 1 mark each for up to three suitable applications; for example solar cells [1], touch panels [1] and smart windows for phones [1].

**Materials: New Materials**

11. 11.1) A material made up of particles that are less than 100 nanometres in size [1].
    11.2) 1 mark for stating an application, and 1 mark for a suitable reason or function. For example, as a coating on fabric [1] to repel dirt, keeping it clean [1].

12. 12.1) Award 1 mark each for any two of: nuts and bolts, screws, hinges, fasteners, caps, washers.
    12.2) Award 1 mark each for any two of: resistors, dual in-line integrated circuit packages (DIL), microcontrollers (for example PICs), capacitors, diodes, LEDs, transistors, switches, motors.
    12.3) Award 1 mark each for any two of: gears, cams, pulleys, belts.

**Finishing Materials**

13. For each material type award 1 mark for each correct finishing type. For example:
    - Paper and board: printing [1], embossing [1]
    - Timber-based materials: painting [1], varnishing [1]
    - Metal-based materials: dip-coating [1], galvanising [1].

14. To improve function and aesthetics [1].

**Selection of Materials**

15. Award 1 mark each for stating two relevant properties and a second mark each for explaining why it is required, up to a maximum of 4 marks. Examples of properties which may be considered include the following.

| | |
|---|---|
| Promotional flyer | Ability to be printed<br>Availability<br>Cost |
| Wooden toy | Aesthetics: colour and texture that appeal to children<br>Absorbency and resistance to corrosion, in case put in child's mouth<br>Toughness, to resist impacts or being dropped<br>Hardness, to resist being scratched or damaged in use |
| Cooking pan | Thermal conductivity, to allow heat through<br>Absorbency and resistance to corrosion, to resist tainting the contents<br>Malleability for ease of manufacture<br>Hardness to avoid being scratched or worn when in use<br>Density, lightweight to lift easily |
| Plastic chair | Compressive strength to support the person sitting on it<br>Absorbency and resistance to corrosion, to resist damage by rain if used outside<br>Density, lightweight so can be lifted easily and put away |
| Football shirt | Aesthetics: colour and texture that appeal to the user<br>Elasticity/stretchiness to provide a good fit/shape<br>Density, lightweight to avoid additional load on wearer |
| Gearbox | Toughness so it does not break on impact in an accident<br>Density, lightweight to reduce fuel requirements<br>Absorbency and resistance to corrosion, so that it doesn't stop working in wet weather<br>Hardness of mechanical parts, so they last a long time before wearing out |

16. Award 1 mark each for stating three methods and a second mark each for describing what it involves or how it provides reinforcement. For example:
    - Bending and folding **[1]** increase the effective thickness of sheet material **[1]**.
    - Lamination **[1]** involves adding layers of material **[1]**.
    - Webbing **[1]** uses ribs of material, normally located on the inside of a product to increase the stiffness.
    - Interfacing **[1]** involves adding extra layers of material to a textile product **[1]**.

## Pages 92–107 Revise Questions

**Page 93 Quick Test**
1. A group of identical products are made together, before changing to making a group of a different product.
2. For example cars, nuts and bolts
3. The standard shapes and sizes in which a material is available

**Page 95 Quick Test**
1. Scissors, scalpels, craft knives, compass cutters and circle cutters, rotary trimmers and guillotines
2. Adding additional layers to a material
3. Screen printing, offset lithography

**Page 97 Quick Test**
1. Tenon, coping, band saw, circular saw (also powered fretsaw and jigsaw)
2. Polyvinyl adhesive (PVA)
3. Steam bending, laminating using a former

**Page 99 Quick Test**
1. Centre lathe
2. Adhesive/epoxy resin, welding, brazing
3. To allow air to escape when the molten metal is poured in

**Page 101 Quick Test**
1. Coping saw, powered fretsaw, band saw
2. Heat from an electrically heated welding gun or a hot plate is used to melt the faces to be joined, which are pushed together to form the joint as they cool.
3. In injection moulding the formed part is solid; in blow moulding, the output from the injection moulding unit is a pipe, which is expanded within the mould using air to create a hollow product.

**Page 103 Quick Test**
1. A strip of adhesive web is placed between the two fabrics. Heat from an iron then fuses them together.
2. Make a single or double fold and add stiches at the top or side to hold it in place.
3. Manual soldering, reflow (flow) soldering.

**Page 105 Quick Test**
1. A reference point for measurement on a material, product or object
2. To ensure accuracy and precision of manufacture.
3. To ensure that all parts of a product are made the same.
4. A type of template that is used to trace the parts of a garment onto fabric before it is cut. Or, a replica of a product to be cast, used to prepare the cavity into which the molten material will be poured.

**Page 107 Quick Test**
1. Accuracy is the degree of closeness of a measurement to its true value, correct value or standard. Precision is how repeatable or reproducible the measurement is.
2. To ensure that a product is fit for purpose.
3. The permissible limits of variation in the dimensions or physical properties of a manufactured product or part.
4. Quality control is product-oriented whereas quality assurance is process-oriented.

## Pages 108–115 Review Questions

**Properties of Materials**
1. 1.1) Hardness **[1]**
   1.2) Thermal conductivity **[1]**

**Materials: Paper and Board**
2. Award marks as indicated, with up to 2 marks for each characteristic and 1 mark for a typical use.

| Type | Characteristics | Typical Use |
|---|---|---|
| Layout and tracing paper | Hard **[1]** and translucent **[1]**<br>Typically 50–90 gsm **[1]** | Working drawings **[1]**, tracing **[1]** |
| Solid white board | Strong **[1]**, white **[1]**<br>Made from pure bleached wood pulp **[1]**<br>200–400 gsm **[1]** | For example book covers **[1]**, expensive packaging **[1]** |
| Corrugated cardboard | Contains two or more layers of card with interlacing fluted inner section **[1]**<br>Often made from recycled material **[1]**, low cost **[1]**<br>From 250 gsm upwards **[1]** | For example boxes **[1]**, packaging **[1]** |
| Foil-lined board | Made by laminating aluminium foil to one side of another board **[1]**<br>Insulating properties **[1]**, can keep moisture in/out **[1]** | For example drinks cartons **[1]**, ready meal lids **[1]** |

## Materials: Timber

3. Award marks as indicated, up to a maximum of 4 marks: hardwoods come from deciduous trees [1] which shed their leaves each autumn [1]. Softwoods come from coniferous trees [1] which keep their leaves all year [1], meaning that they typically grow faster than hardwoods [1]. Softwoods also tend to have a more open grain than hardwoods [1].

4. Award up to 4 marks as follows (information can be in either sketches or notes): trees are cut down [1] and layers of veneer/ plies are shaved from them [1]. These are glued together [1] with the grain structure at 90° to each other [1].

## Materials: Metal

5. 5.1) A mixture of two or more metals [1]
   5.2) i) For example stainless steel [1], high-speed steel [1]
   ii) 1 mark for any of: (for stainless steel) kitchen equipment, medical instruments or any other suitable application; (for HSS) drill bits, saw blades.
   iii) 1 mark each for identifying a requirement of the application and justifying the choice with respect to one of the material properties (for example tough, strong, hard, difficult to machine, corrosion resistant).
   5.3) i) Any suitable non-ferrous alloy, for example brass [1]
   ii) 1 mark for any appropriate application.
   iii) 1 mark each for identifying a requirement of the application and justifying the choice with respect to one of the material properties.

## Materials: Polymers

6. Award marks as indicated up to a maximum of 10 marks: most polymers are made from carbon-based fossil fuels [1] such as oil, gas and coal [1]. These are a finite resource [1] and non-renewable: once they are used they are gone [1]. The extraction of these resources and their transportation can also cause damage to the environment [1]. Sustainable polymers are being developed from vegetable products [1], such as corn starch [1]. Synthetic polymers are not normally biodegradable [1]. At the end of their usable life, thermosetting polymers typically end up in landfill [1], which uses up valuable land [1] and can be a cause of pollution [1] and damage to local habitats [1]. Thermoforming polymers can be recycled [1]. They are normally marked with a symbol to identify their type [1] and they must be sorted before recycling [1]. Any other appropriate response.

## Materials: Textiles

7. Natural fibres come from animals or plants [1], whereas synthetic fibres are made by people, usually from oil [1].
8. 8.1) Home use = 12% of £40 million = 0.12 × 40 = £4.8 million [1 mark for method, 1 mark for answer]

   8.2) Clothing = $\frac{15}{100} = \frac{3}{20}$ [1]

## New Materials and Standard Components

9. A material made by combining two or more different materials [1] where the two materials remain physically distinct within the structure/ are not combined chemically/are only joined mechanically [1].
10. 10.1) Award marks as follows:
    Cost of polymer = 0.4 × £3 = £1.20 [1]
    Total cost = £1.20 + (8 × 0.02) + (2 × 0.32) = £2.00 [1 mark for method, 1 mark for answer]
    10.2) Award marks as follows:
    Total cost = £2 + £2.48 + £1.72 = £6.20 / product [1]
    Allowing for 20% profit, selling price = cost × 1.2 = £7.50 per product [1 mark for method, 1 mark for answer]

## Finishing Materials

11. For each material type award 1 mark for each correct finishing type. For example:
    - polymers: polishing [1], vinyl decals [1]
    - textile-based materials: printing [1], dyeing [1]
    - electronic and mechanical systems: PCB lacquering [1], lubrication [1].

## Selection of Materials

12. Award 1 mark each for up to six of the following: functionality, aesthetics, environmental considerations, availability of materials, cost, social factors, ethical considerations, cultural factors.
13. Award 1 mark for stating the modification and 1 mark for stating how this will affect the properties of the material. For example:
    - Paper and board: additives [1] can be added to prevent moisture transfer [1].
    - Timber: seasoning [1] can reduce warping [1], increase strength [1] and hardness [1].
    - Metal alloys: annealing [1] can be used to increase the malleability [1]; anodizing [1] can improve the hardness of aluminium [1].
    - Polymers: chemical additives [1] can reduce UV degradation [1].
    - Textiles: flame retardants [1] reduce fire hazards by making the fabric more difficult to set on fire [1].
    - PCB board: photosensitive board [1] can be used to mask areas that have been exposed to light when the board is etched by chemicals [1].

## Working with Materials

14. Award 1 mark each for any of: using a stronger material, increasing the thickness of a material, bending or folding, laminating, use of webbing, interfacing.

## Pages 116–121 Practice Questions

### Scales of Manufacture, and Manufacturing Processes 1 and 2

1. Award 1 mark for each suitable example given. For example: one off: tailored suit, satellites; batch: furniture, clothes for high street stores; mass: chocolate bars, bottles, cars; continuous: steel, oil, chemicals.
2. Award marks as follows: metal blades are positioned in the shape to be cut [1]. They are pushed into the card [1]. Foam rubber around the blade compresses during cutting and pushes to release the cut material [1].
3. a) Making straight cuts [1]
   b) Reducing the size of a piece of timber [1]
   c) Creating deep holes for joints [1]
   d) Turning a round section [1]
   e) Planing end grain [1]
   f) Making grooves and edge profiles [1]
4. Laminating [1], steam bending [1].
5. Horizontal paring cleans out unwanted material [1] by cutting across a joint [1], whereas vertical paring shapes the end of a piece of wood [1] by pushing down onto the waste surface [1].

### Manufacturing Processes 3: Metals and Alloys

6. Metal shears [1], guillotine [1].
7. Award up to 3 marks as follows (information can be in either sketches or notes): the work piece is held in a chuck [1] and rotated [1]. The cutting tool is moved into the workpiece [1]; it can be moved left and right along the length and in or out to achieve different radii [1].
8. Award up to a maximum of 4 marks as follows: a reusable metal mould is made [1]. Molten metal is poured into a cylinder/into the die-casting machine [1]. A ram then forces this metal into the mould [1]. Pressure is held until the metal solidifies and cools [1]. The mould is then opened and the component removed [1].

### Manufacturing Processes 4: Polymers

9. 9.1) Award marks as follows: the faces to be joined are heated [1] using an electrically heated welding gun or a hot plate [1]. When these melt [1] they pushed together [1], forming the joint as they cool [1].
   9.2) Solvent cement [1].
10. Award marks as follows (information can be in either sketches or notes): a thermoplastic sheet is heated in an oven until it is flexible [1]. It is then pressed between two moulds [1]. The moulds are male mould and female yoke [1]. It is allowed to cool and hardens into the shape of the mould [1].

# Answers

**Manufacturing Processes 5: Textiles and Electronic Systems**

11. 11.1) Award 1 mark each for any two of: rotary cutter, scissors, pinking shears.

    11.2) Award marks as follows: it allows a garment to increase fullness or widen out, modifying the shape [1]. It allows a longer piece of fabric to be attached within the length of a shorter piece [1]

    11.3) Award up to two marks as follows: quilting creates surface texture [1] by sandwiching wadding or stuffing between layers of fabric [1] and stitching through the layers [1].

12. Award up to 4 marks as follows: the component is placed through the holes in the circuit board, legs to the copper track side [1]. A small amount of solder is applied to the soldering iron, called 'tinning' [1]. The soldering iron is used to heat the point where the component comes through the board for 2–3 seconds [1]. Solder is fed onto the heated area [1] where it melts and forms the joint [1].

**Measurement and Production Aids, and Ensuring Accuracy**

13. 9–12 marks: thorough knowledge and understanding of how accuracy can be ensured when manufacturing products. All points fully explained. Several relevant examples presented to support answer. 5–8 marks: good knowledge and understanding of how accuracy can be ensured when manufacturing products. Majority of points explained. Some relevant examples presented to support answer. 1–4 marks: limited knowledge or understanding. Mainly descriptive response. Few or no relevant examples presented to support answer.

    Indicative answer: accurate measuring and marking out results in parts/products that are cut more accurately. Datums should also be worked to. Tools such as jigs, templates and patterns can be used to ensure accuracy. For example, a jig can be set up to hold and guide a drill, thus ensuring holes are drilled in the same place on each piece of material. A template can be drawn round to ensure a part is produced exactly the same each time it is cut. Tolerances are shown on drawings and/or specifications. They should be followed to ensure the product/part is produced within these permissible limits of variation.

## Pages 122–127 Revise Questions

### Page 123 Quick Test

1. A way for people to raise awareness and money for a project or idea, where people donate money in return for rewards
2. A business or organisation that is run jointly by and for the benefit of its members
3. Less employment for people/change in job roles/retraining of staff to fill different roles

### Page 125 Quick Test

1. Computer-aided design, computer-aided manufacture
2. An approach to improve efficiency of manufacture through the elimination of waste
3. Technology push is where products are developed because of new materials or technologies becoming available, whereas market pull is where products are developed due to market forces.

### Page 127 Quick Test

1. Finite resources are resources that will eventually run out. Non-finite resources are resources that are easy to replenish.
2. Through efficient working practices
3. So that products do not cause offence or upset

## Pages 128–133 Review Questions

### Scales of Manufacture, and Manufacturing Processes 1 and 2

1. 1.1) Award marks as indicated: a group of identical products are made together [1], followed by other groups of similar (but not necessarily identical) products [1].

    1.2) Award 1 mark each for three suitable examples. For example chairs, tables, clothes for high street stores, fire extinguishers, etc.

2. Award marks as follows up to a maximum of 5 marks (information can be in either sketches or notes). The image to print is in relief on the printing plate [1]. Ink is applied, which is attracted to the image [1]. The plate is dampened, which repels ink from any non-image areas [1]. The printing plate transfers an inked image onto the rubber blanket cylinder [1]. The rubber blanket cylinder presses the image onto the paper or card as it's fed through [1].

3. Award 1 mark each for stating three safety precautions and 1 mark each for stating three relevant hazards. For example:
   - eye goggles [1] to protect against swarf/flying debris [1]
   - machine guard [1] to protect against entanglement in the rotating chuck [1]
   - spring-loaded chuck key [1] so this is not accidentally left in the machine and ejected in use [1]
   - using a machine vice or clamp to hold the workpiece [1] to stop it spinning and cutting the user [1].

4. Award up to 5 marks as follows: the timber is heated in steam [1] until it becomes pliable [1]. It is then shaped round a former [1]. It must be clamped in place until it is cool [1] when it will retain the shape of the former [1].

**Manufacturing Processes 3: Metals and Alloys**

5. Award 1 mark each for two of: manual bending using a former; feeding the sheet between rollers moving at different speeds; using a press.

6.
   a) Hacksaw [1]
   b) Centre lathe [1]
   c) Drill [1]
   d) Milling machine [1]

7. Award marks as indicated up to a maximum of 4 marks: die casting uses a reusable metal mould [1] which is much more expensive than a mould made from sand [1]. Even though in sand casting a new mould has to be made every time [1], for a batch of 10 products the total cost will probably be less than the cost of the metal mould [1]. Further, the equipment cost for sand casting is much less than for die casting [1].

**Manufacturing Processes 4: Polymers**

8. Award 1 mark each for two of: coping saw, (powered) fretsaw, jigsaw, band saw.

9. Award up to 4 marks as follows: a CAD model of the product is produced [1]; this is split into multiple layers by a computer [1]; the 3D printer deposits one layer of material [1], then moves up to deposit the next layer, until the product is complete [1].

10. Award up to 4 marks as follows: a split mould is made in the shape of the bottle [1]. Air is blown into an extruded section of plastic tube [1]. The air forces plastic to the sides of the mould [1]. The mould is then cooled and the product is removed [1].

**Manufacturing Processes 5: Textiles and Electronic Systems**

11. To provide a professional finish to seams and hems/to provide a decorative finish [1].

12. Award up to 4 marks as follows: it is used to apply patterns or images to long lengths of fabric [1]. Ink is applied to a series of different rollers in contact with the fabric [1]. Each roller has a pattern/image and normally applies a different colour [1]. The fabric moves continuously [1].

13. Award up to 6 marks as follows: in manual soldering, components are pushed through the circuit board [1] and heat is applied by a soldering iron [1] before the solder is added [1]. The soldered joint is formed on the reverse of the circuit board [1]. In flow soldering components are mounted on top of the circuit board [1] after solder paste is applied [1] and the whole assembly is heated [1]. The soldered joint is formed on the same side of the circuit board as the component [1].

**Measurement and Production Aids, and Ensuring Accuracy**

**14. 14.1)** Up to 2 marks for each definition.
- Jig: a custom tool **[1]** for making sure parts of a product are exactly the same **[1]**.
- Tolerance: the permissible limits of variation **[1]** in the dimensions of a manufactured product **[1]**.

**14.2)** Up to 3 marks for explanation. For example: failure to use tolerances could result in improper fits **[1]**, which would result in the product being rejected by clients/ stakeholders **[1]**. This would add extra cost and time as the product would need to be remade **[1]**.

## Pages 134–135 Practice Questions

**Impact on Industry, and Impact on Society and Environment**

**1. 1.1)** 1 mark for correct answer: a.

**1.2)** Up to 2 marks for explanation and 1 mark for suitable example. For example: so as not to cause offence/confusion **[1]** as some colours/logos/symbols mean different things in different cultures **[1]**. For example, red is considered good luck in China but symbolises danger in western cultures **[1]**.

**1.3)** Up to 2 marks for explanation of one benefit. For example: reduction in time taken to manufacture products **[1]** due to reducing waiting time/time when no activity is taking place **[1]**.

**Impact on Production**

**2.** 1 mark for each suitable advantage and disadvantage. For example:
- Advantages: increased accuracy of design **[1]**, easier to make changes to design **[1]**, complex designs can be created quickly **[1]**.
- Disadvantages: initial cost of software can be high **[1]**, requires access to suitable ICT hardware **[1]**.

## Pages 136–137 Review Questions

**Impact on Industry, and Impact on Society and Environment**

**1. 1.1)** 1 mark for each advantage and 1 mark for any suitable disadvantage. For example:
- Advantages: increased efficiency **[1]**, better product quality **[1]**.
- Disadvantage: reduced employment opportunities for people **[1]**.

**1.2)** Up to 2 marks for description of difference. For example: finite resources are non-renewable/will run out **[1]**. Non-finite resources are renewable/will not run out **[1]**.

**Impact on Production**

**2.** 1 mark for each suitable advantage and disadvantage. For example:
- Advantages: consistency of production **[1]**, high levels of manufacturing accuracy **[1]**, high speed of manufacture **[1]**.
- Disadvantages: initial cost of machinery can be high **[1]**, time/ cost of training staff to use machinery **[1]**.

## Pages 138–147 Mix Exam-Style Questions

**1. 1.1)** Award marks as follows up to a maximum of 5 marks (information can be in either sketches or notes): plastic powder or granules are fed from a hopper into the machine **[1]**. Heaters melt the plastic **[1]**. A screw moves the plastic along towards the mould **[1]**. The screw provides pressure on the plastic, forcing it into the mould **[1]**. Pressure is maintained on the mould until it has cooled enough to be opened **[1]**.

**1.2)** Material needed = 20 000 × 2.4 × $10^{-5}$ = 0.48 m³ **[1]**; material lost = 0.5 – 0.48 = 0.02 m³ or 20 × $10^{-3}$ m³ **[1]**

**1.3)** Profit = 8.00 – 6.40 = £1.60 **[1]**; % profit = 1.60 / 8.00 × 100/1 = 20% **[1]**

**2.** Award marks as follows up to a maximum of 10 marks (information can be in either sketches or notes). A pattern is made, normally in wood **[1]**. This is sandwiched between two boxes of oiled sand **[1]**. The boxes are called the cope and the drag **[1]**. The sand is compressed around the pattern **[1]**. The cope and drag are carefully separated and the pattern removed, leaving a hollow shape when they are reassembled **[1]**. There will be a hole for a runner, to allow the metal to be poured in **[1]**. There will also be a hole for a riser, to let air escape **[1]**. The metal is melted **[1]**. Metal is poured in through the runner **[1]**. Once the metal has cooled, the sand mould can be broken/shaken off **[1]**. The runner and riser can be cut off **[1]**. Any excess metal/flash will be removed and the casting trimmed or cleaned by fettling **[1]**.

**3. a)** Award 1 mark for tenon saw.
**b)** Award 1 mark for cutting circles.
**c)** Award 1 mark for metal.
**d)** Award 1 mark for paper and card.
**e)** Award 1 mark for cutting straight lines.
**f)** Award 1 mark for pinking shears.
**g)** Award 1 mark for centre lathe.

**4. 4.1)** 1 mark for each appropriate input and output, such as LDR (input) and lamp (output).

**4.2)** Up to 2 marks for each reason explained. For example: a single microcontroller could replace a whole timing circuit **[1]**, leading to a smaller product **[1]**. Microcontrollers can be reprogrammed **[1]**, so the time period of the light could be shortened if the child gets less scared of the dark **[1]**.

**5. a)** Push–pull linkage **[1]**
**b)** Rotary **[1]**
**c)** Linear **[1]**
**d)** Reciprocating **[1]**

**6.** Award up to 6 marks as follows: spur gears would allow greater torque **[1]**, as with a pulley and belt high torque may cause the belt to slip **[1]**. The pulley and belt may weigh less than the gears **[1]** as the gears would have to be large enough to mesh/ touch **[1]** whereas the pulleys could be small and only connected by the belt **[1]**. The belt on the pulley system could stretch to absorb shocks **[1]**, which could otherwise damage the gears **[1]**. The pulley and belt may be easier to manufacture than the gears **[1]**, which could mean that it costs less **[1]**. Any other appropriate response.

**7. 7.1)** Up to 4 marks for explanation. For example: make the product easy to disassemble **[1]** so that the materials/ components could be reused in a different product **[1]**. Make the product easy to repair **[1]** so it does not have to be thrown away when a component fails **[1]**.

**7.2)** Up to 2 marks for correct definition. For example: the total distance that a product travels **[1]** from its place of manufacture to where it is used **[1]**.

**7.3)** Up to 2 marks for explanation. For example: oceanic pollution can cause death to marine life **[1]** as a result of the harmful chemicals/industrial waste being deposited there **[1]**.

**8. a)** Reciprocating **[1]**
**b)** Oscillating **[1]**
**c)** Rotary **[1]**
**d)** Linear **[1]**

**9. 9.1)** Second order **[1]**
**9.2)** Mechanical advantage = (40 + 80) / 40 = 3 [1 mark for method, 1 mark for correct answer]

**10. 10.1)** Suppliers deliver materials only when they are needed/ about to be used **[1]**.

**10.2)** Reduces the amount of storage space needed **[1]**; less chance of stock being damaged **[1]**; less wasted materials **[1]**.

**11.** Award marks as follows up to a maximum of 5 marks (information can be in either sketches or notes). Plastic powder or granules are fed from a hopper into the machine **[1]**. Heaters melt the plastic **[1]**. A screw moves the plastic along towards the mould **[1]**. The screw provides pressure on the plastic, turning it into a continuous stream [1]. The pressure forces the plastic through a die in the profile of the tube, creating the pipe [1].

12. 1 mark for each computer-based tool. Up to 2 marks for explanation of use of each. For example: CAD software [1]: used to create 3D models of products [1] which allows them to be simulated before a physical prototype is produced [1]. Presentation software [1]: used to present initial design ideas to the client [1] so they can give feedback [1].

13. 13.1) Up to 2 marks for each advantage and any disadvantage explained. For example:
- Advantage 1: less storage space is needed [1] as raw materials are only purchased when they are needed [1].
- Advantage 2: waste is reduced [1] as materials are not damaged while in storage [1].
- Disadvantage: there is a risk that raw materials will run out [1] as not as much is kept in storage [1].

13.2) Up to 2 marks for explanation of purpose. For example: to reduce waste [1] by eliminating activities that consume resources without adding value [1].

# Glossary

**Absorbency**   the ability of a material to draw in moisture

**Accuracy**   the degree of closeness of a measurement to its true value

**Adhesive**   a chemical used to stick or glue objects together

**Aesthetics**   how a product appeals to the five senses; its sense of beauty

**Alloy**   a mixture of two or more metals

**Annotation**   adding labels identifying and explaining key features on a drawing

**Anthropometric data**   measurements taken from millions of people of different shapes and sizes and placed in charts

**Art Nouveau**   a design movement known for its use of long, organic lines and architectural designs

**Arts and Crafts**   a design movement that favoured a return to traditional craft methods

**Atmospheric pollution**   the release of pollutants into the Earth's atmosphere

**Automation**   the use of computer systems and control technology to operate equipment

**Batch production**   making a series of groups of identical products

**Battery**   converts chemical energy to electrical energy to power products and systems

**Bauhaus**   a German design school that existed from 1919 to 1933 and favoured a minimalist approach to design

**Biodegradable**   the ability to decompose or rot due to interaction with the environment

**Biomass**   fuel that is developed from organic materials, such as crops, scrap wood and animal waste

**Blow moulding**   a process used to shape hollow polymer products

**Bonding**   a method of joining fabrics without stitching

**Brazing**   a joining process for metals where a joint is created by soldering at high temperature

**Breadboarding**   a temporary, physical method for prototyping electronic circuits

**Cam**   a mechanism that converts rotary motion to reciprocating motion

**Casting**   pouring molten metal into a mould to form a product

**CNC**   computer numerical control; using a computer to control a machine tool

**Composite**   a material made up of two or more other materials that are not chemically combined

**Computer-aided design (CAD)**   the use of computer software to produce designs for products

**Computer-aided manufacture (CAM)**   the use of computer software to control machine tools to manufacture products

**Continuous improvement**   a process where ongoing incremental improvements are made to a product or system

**Continuous production**   making a material or chemical continuously using dedicated equipment

**Co-operative**   a business or organisation that is run jointly by and for the benefit of its members

**Cracking**   a process where complex organic chemicals are broken down into simpler molecules such as the monomers used to make polymers

**Crowd funding**   a way for people to raise awareness and money for a project or idea, where people donate money in return for rewards

**Datum surface**   a reference point for measurement on a material, product or object

**Deforestation**   the removal of forests and conversion of the land to other uses

**Density**   mass of material per unit volume

**Design brief**   a short description of a design problem and how it is to be solved

**Design fixation**   when designers become overly attached to a particular idea, therefore not taking account of other potential solutions

**Design specification**   a list of measurable design criteria that a product or system must meet

**De Stijl**   a Dutch design movement that simplified designs by using only horizontal and vertical lines, and primary colours

**Die casting**   a process where molten metal is shaped using pressure and a reusable mould

**Die cutting**   a process that uses metal blades and a press to cut a shape in paper or card

**Ductility**   the ability of a material to be stretched without breaking and stay permanently in its new form

**Economies of scale**   a saving in cost per product gained by making a higher number of products

**Effort**   the force applied to something (for example to a lever)

**Elasticity**   the ability of a material to return to its original shape when a force on it is removed

**Electrical conductivity**   the ability of electricity to be conducted by a material

**Electronic system**   a collection of input, process, driver and output stages that respond to, change and produce different types of signals

**Embossing**   a technique that uses steel dies to press a shape onto the material, giving a tactile effect

**End user**   the person or people that will use a product when it is completed

**Ergonomics**   the study of how people interact with the products and systems around them

**Evaluation**   an assessment of how well a product or prototype looks, functions or does its job

**Exploded drawing**   a picture that shows how the parts of a product fit together

**Extrusion**   making a sectional shape by pushing material through a die

**Fair trade**   a movement that works to help people in developing countries get a fair deal for the products that they produce

**'Fast fashion'**   a trend where catwalk clothing designs move quickly to the high street so people can capture the current fashions; often clothes will only be worn for a single 'season' before being replaced

**Ferrous metal**   a metal that contains iron

**Finite resource**   a resource of which there is only a limited quantity

**Former**   a profiled shape used to mould material

**Fossil fuel**   fuel created from the remains of dead organisms over a long period of time; for example, coal, oil and gas

**Fractional distillation**   separation of a liquid mixture into the different chemicals of which it is comprised by a chemical distillation process

**Fulcrum**   the pivot point of a lever

**Functionality**   how well a product fulfils the purpose it is designed to meet

**Fusibility**   the ability of a material to be changed from a solid to a liquid by heat

**Gathering**   a sewing technique for shortening the length of a strip of fabric, to allow a longer piece to be attached to a shorter piece

**Gear**   a mechanism used to transfer rotary motion, which can also change the direction or magnitude of the force transmitted

**Grain**   the growth rings visible on the surface of the wood

**Graphene**   a form of carbon consisting of sheets which are one atom thick

**gsm**   grams per square metre; the weight of paper or card

**Hardness**   the resistance of a material to wear and abrasion

**Hardwood**   wood from deciduous trees that shed their leaves each autumn

**Hydro-electrical energy**   energy that is taken from flowing water, typically by releasing water from a dam to turn turbines

# Glossary

**Inclusive design**   the design of products and systems that can be used by everyone, without any special adaptations
**Injection moulding**   a process used to shape polymer products
**Input device**   a device that turns a real-world signal, such as light, sound or movement, into an electronic signal
**Interfacing**   adding multiple layers of material to a textile product to increase its strength
**Isometric projection**   a scaled 3D drawing with sides at an angle of 30° to the baseline
**Iterative design**   a cyclic design approach where each iteration is tested, evaluated and refined, resulting in a new iteration

**Jig**   a custom-made tool designed to achieve accuracy, repeatability and interchangeability during product manufacture
**Just-in-time production**   a production technique where suppliers deliver materials only when they are needed

**Knitted**   made from yarn using interlocking loops

**Laminating**   overlaying a flat object or sheet of material with a layer of protective material
**Lean manufacturing**   an approach to improve efficiency of manufacture through the elimination of waste
**Lever**   a simple device that pivots about a fulcrum
**Linear**   moving in a straight line
**Line bending**   a process that involves bending thermoplastic along a heated line
**Linkage**   an assembly of parts used to transfer motion between two mechanisms, which can also change the direction or magnitude of the force transmitted

**Malleability**   the ability of a material for its shape to be permanently changed without the material breaking
**Manufacturing specification**   a set of information that is required to manufacture a product or system
**Market pull**   products developed because of market forces
**Market research**   when information is collected to find out whether there is a place in the market for a proposed product
**Mass production**   making the same product in large quantities
**Mathematical model**   a representation of a product or system using mathematical formulae
**Memphis**   a design movement characterised by the use of asymmetric shapes and colourful decoration
**Metal foam**   a metal containing gas-filled pores, giving it a very low density
**Microcontroller**   a small, programmable computer on a chip that is designed for use in control applications
**Model**   a representation of a product or system that is being developed
**Moisture-wicking fabric**   fabric that removes sweat from the skin and carries it to the outside of the fabric
**Moulding**   using a former to shape a material

**Nanomaterials**   materials made up of particles that are less than 100 nanometres in size
**Natural fibres**   fibres from sources such as animals and plants
**Non-ferrous metal**   a metal that does not contain iron
**Non-renewable energy source**   an energy source that cannot replenish itself quickly and therefore will eventually run out
**Nuclear power**   power that is created by making use of highly controlled nuclear reactions, such as nuclear fission

**Oceanic pollution**   the release of chemicals or industrial waste into the oceans
**Offset lithography**   a transfer printing process used to print products in large quantities

**One-off/bespoke production**   making a single product to a customer specification
**Orthographic projection**   a scale drawing that shows a series of views of a part
**Oscillating**   swinging in alternate directions
**Output device**   a device that turns an electronic signal into a real-world signal, such as light or sound

**Pattern**   a type of template that is used to trace the parts of a garment onto fabric before it is cut; also, a replica of a product to be cast, used to prepare the cavity into which the molten material will be poured
**PCB lacquering**   the application of a waterproof and protective layer for the tracks and pads of a printed circuit board (PCB)
**Perforation**   a hole in a material
**Perspective**   a 3D drawing technique that uses guidelines to show how dimensions change with distance
**Piping**   a strip of folded over fabric inserted in a seam in a textile product
**Pleating**   making a double or multiple fold in a textile product, held by stitching
**Ply**   a layer of paper, wood or fabric in a material
**Polishing**   a finishing technique used to protect and improve the aesthetics of plastics and metals
**Polymer**   a material made from chains of a repeating chemical part called a monomer
**Precision**   how repeatable or reproducible a measurement is
**Presentation software**   software that allows visual aids to be created for face-to-face presentations
**Pressing**   applying pressure to deform a material
**Primary data**   raw data taken first hand or from original research
**Process**   changes an electronic signal to create functions such as timing and counting
**Prototype**   a full-sized, actual version or primary example of an intended product or system
**Pulley**   a mechanism comprising two wheels linked by a belt; this transfers rotary motion and can also change the direction or magnitude of the force transmitted

**Quality assurance**   putting systems in place that ensure the quality of the processes used to manufacture the product
**Quality control**   testing and checking that a product meets the specification or a set of defined quality standards
**Quilting**   sandwiching wadding or stuffing between layers of fabric and stitching through the layers

**Reciprocating**   moving backwards and forwards
**Recycle**   to reprocess or convert waste back into a useful material
**Reinforcement**   adding strength or stiffness to a product
**Renewable energy source**   a source that can replenish itself quickly and therefore will not run out
**Rotating**   turning in a circle

**Scale**   the ratio of the size of a drawn object to the size of the object
**Secondary data**   data that is freely available and taken from other parties or sources
**Selvedge**   an edge of a fabric that will not fray
**Sewing**   a method of joining fabrics by stitching with thread
**Shearing**   a wasting process used to cut material
**Softwood**   wood from trees that maintain their foliage all year round
**Solar energy**   energy that is taken from the sun, typically by using solar panels to harness sunlight and convert it into electricity
**Soldering**   a joining process for metals where a filler metal is melted to join parts together

**Spreadsheet software** software that presents and allows the analysis of data in tabular form

**Standard component** a common part that is commercially available in specified sizes

**Stock forms** the standard shapes and sizes in which a material is available

**Strength** the ability of a material to withstand a force that is applied to it

**Sustainable** naturally replenished within a short period of time

**Synthetic** made by people; not natural

**Synthetic fibres** fibres made by people, typically from oil or chemicals

**Systems thinking** a top-down design approach that starts with an overview of the overall system in terms of its input, process and output sub-systems

**Technical textile** a fabric made for its performance properties rather than aesthetic characteristics

**Technology push** products developed as a result of developments in materials and/or manufacturing technologies/techniques

**Template** used to draw a shape onto material which can then be cut around

**Thermal conductivity** the ability of heat to be conducted through a material

**Thermoforming polymer** a polymer that can be reshaped when it is heated

**Thermosetting polymer** a polymer that will not change its shape when reheated

**Toile** an early version of a piece of clothing, usually made from cheap materials

**Tolerance** the permissible limits of variation in the dimensions or physical properties of a manufactured product or part

**Toughness** the ability of a material to absorb an impact without rupturing

**Trend** a change in direction in the way people are acting or behaving

**Turning** using a lathe to create a product with a round profile by wasting

**User-centred design** a design approach where the needs and wants of the end user are considered extensively at each stage of the design process

**Vacuum forming** a process where heated plastic is formed onto a mould using a vacuum

**Varnishing** a finishing technique for timber where varnish is applied to protect the wood underneath

**Veneer** a thin layer of wood

**Virtual meeting software** software that allows face-to-face meetings to occur between people in different locations over a wired, wireless or mobile network

**Wasting** removal of material

**Webbing** ribs of material that provide reinforcement, normally inside a product

**Welding** a joining process for materials where the parts are melted along the joint line by heat

**Wind energy** energy that is taken from the wind, typically by using wind turbines to generate electricity

**Working drawing** a scale drawing that shows the dimensions of a part

**Woven** made from interlaced yarn

**Yarn** spun and twisted fibres

# Index

# Collins

# AQA GCSE 9-1
# Design and Technology

*Workbook*

Paul Anderson and David Hills-Taylor

# Contents

## Tools, Equipment and Processes

## New and Emerging Technologies

# Design Strategies

**1** The table shows three design strategies.

Complete the table by giving **one** advantage and **one** disadvantage of using each design strategy.

| Design Approach | Advantage of Strategy | Disadvantage of Strategy |
| --- | --- | --- |
| Iterative design | | |
| User-centred design | | |
| Systems thinking | | |

[6]

Total Marks .............. / 6

# Electronic Systems

**1** The table shows different electronic components.

Complete the table by stating whether each component is an input, process or output device and giving an example application of each in a product.

| Component | Input, Process or Output | Application |
|---|---|---|
| Push switch | | |
| Lamp | | |
| Microcontroller | | |
| Thermistor | | |
| Buzzer | | |

[10]

Total Marks _____ / 10

# The Work of Others: Designers

**1** Name a designer you have studied.

.......................................................................................................................................................... [1]

**2** State a product that the designer given in your answer to question 1 has designed.

.......................................................................................................................................................... [1]

**3** Give **four** features of the design given in your answer to question 2.

1 ........................................................................................................................................................

........................................................................................................................................................

2 ........................................................................................................................................................

........................................................................................................................................................

3 ........................................................................................................................................................

........................................................................................................................................................

4 ........................................................................................................................................................

.......................................................................................................................................................... [4]

Total Marks .................. / 6

# The Work of Others: Companies

**1** Name a design company that you have studied.

............................................................................................................................................................ [1]

**2** State a product that the company given in your answer to question 1 has designed.

............................................................................................................................................................ [1]

**3** Give **four** features of the design given in your answer to question 2.

1 ............................................................................................................................................................

............................................................................................................................................................

2 ............................................................................................................................................................

............................................................................................................................................................

3 ............................................................................................................................................................

............................................................................................................................................................

4 ............................................................................................................................................................

............................................................................................................................................................ [4]

Total Marks ............ / 6

# Ecological, Environmental and Social Issues

1. Explain **three** ways that a product can be designed to be more sustainable.

1 ................................................................................................................................................................................

................................................................................................................................................................................

................................................................................................................................................................................

................................................................................................................................................................................

2 ................................................................................................................................................................................

................................................................................................................................................................................

................................................................................................................................................................................

................................................................................................................................................................................

3 ................................................................................................................................................................................

................................................................................................................................................................................

................................................................................................................................................................................

................................................................................................................................................................................

[6]

2. The image shows the Fairtrade Certification mark.

What is meant by the term 'fair trade'?

................................................................................................................................................................................

................................................................................................................................................................................

................................................................................................................................................................................

[2]

# Research and Investigation

**1** Explain why designers conduct market research.

.....................................................................................................................................................

.....................................................................................................................................................

.....................................................................................................................................................

.....................................................................................................................................................

..................................................................................................................................... [2]

**2** Explain the purpose of a focus group.

.....................................................................................................................................................

.....................................................................................................................................................

.....................................................................................................................................................

.....................................................................................................................................................

..................................................................................................................................... [2]

**3** Give **two** types of data that can be used when investigating a design problem.

1 .................................................................................................................................................

2 ............................................................................................................................................. [2]

**4** Which of the following is the correct definition of anthropometric data? Tick **one** correct box.

   **a** Height measurements taken from a small sample of people. ☐

   **b** A range of body measurements taken from large numbers of people. ☐

   **c** A range of body measurements taken from a small sample of people. ☐

   **d** Head measurements taken from millions of people. ☐ [1]

> **Total Marks** .................. / 7

# Briefs and Specifications

**1** A design brief for a new product is shown.

> **Design brief**
>
> Young children learn about the world around them through play.
>
> A local company is designing an educational toy aimed at children aged 4–7.
>
> The toy must help the children to improve their literacy skills.

Write a **three**-point design specification for a product that would meet the design brief.

Explain why each point is important.

1 ...............................................................................................................................................

...............................................................................................................................................

Explanation .............................................................................................................................

...............................................................................................................................................

...............................................................................................................................................

2 ...............................................................................................................................................

...............................................................................................................................................

Explanation .............................................................................................................................

...............................................................................................................................................

...............................................................................................................................................

3 ...............................................................................................................................................

...............................................................................................................................................

Explanation .............................................................................................................................

...............................................................................................................................................

...............................................................................................................................................

[6]

Total Marks ............... / 6

# Exploring and Developing Ideas

**1** Sketching ideas can be one stage of an iterative design process.

Give **four** other possible stages of an iterative design process.

1 .................................................................................................................................................

2 .................................................................................................................................................

3 .................................................................................................................................................

4 ...........................................................................................................................................  **[4]**

**2** The image shows a freehand sketch of a product idea.

Explain why designers produce freehand sketches of ideas for products.

.................................................................................................................................................

.................................................................................................................................................

.................................................................................................................................................

.................................................................................................................................................

.................................................................................................................................................

.................................................................................................................................................

.................................................................................................................................................

...........................................................................................................................................  **[4]**

# Communication of Ideas 1

**1** State the purpose of an exploded view drawing.

.......................................................................................................................................

.......................................................................................................................................　[1]

**2** A company has asked you to design a stand for a mobile phone.

**2.1)**　On the grid, produce an isometric drawing of your design idea.　[4]

**2.2)**　Annotate your design to indicate the main features, including:

- the materials and finishes to be used

- how it could be made.

[4]

Total Marks ................ / 9

# Communication of Ideas 2

**1** An alarm system has the following features: when a door is opened, this is detected by a switch. This starts a siren, which stays on for 5 minutes.

Draw a systems diagram for the alarm system, labelling each of the systems blocks and signals.

[12]

**2** Explain why a designer may use card to make a physical model of a product.

1 ................................................................................................................................................

2 ................................................................................................................................................ [2]

Total Marks _____ / 14

# Computer-Based Tools

**1** Tick the correct box. CAD means:

    **a)** Computer-aided drawing ☐

    **b)** Computer-assisted drawing ☐

    **c)** Computer-aided design ☐

    **d)** Computer-assisted drawing ☐ **[1]**

**2** Tick the correct box. CAM means:

    **a)** Computer-aided manufacture ☐

    **b)** Computer-assisted manufacture ☐

    **c)** Computer-aided making ☐

    **d)** Computer-assisted making ☐ **[1]**

**3** State **four** different ways in which CAD software can be used during the process of developing a product.

1 .................................................................................................................................................

2 .................................................................................................................................................

3 .................................................................................................................................................

4 ................................................................................................................................................. **[4]**

> **Total Marks** .................... / 6

# Prototype Development

**1** State **four** reasons why a designer might make a prototype of a product.

1 ................................................................................................................................

................................................................................................................................

2 ................................................................................................................................

................................................................................................................................

3 ................................................................................................................................

................................................................................................................................

4 ................................................................................................................................

................................................................................................................................ **[4]**

**2** Explain how a prototype may be different to the final product.

................................................................................................................................

................................................................................................................................

................................................................................................................................

................................................................................................................................

................................................................................................................................

................................................................................................................................

................................................................................................................................

................................................................................................................................

................................................................................................................................

................................................................................................................................ **[6]**

**Total Marks** ............... / 10

**Designing Products**

# Energy Generation and Storage

**1** The table shows different sources of energy.

Complete the table by stating whether each is renewable or non-renewable and describing how each is used to produce energy.

| Source of Energy | Renewable or Non-Renewable | Description of How Energy is Produced |
|---|---|---|
| Tidal | | |
| Coal | | |

[6]

**2** Explain **one** advantage and **one** disadvantage of using nuclear power to generate energy.

Advantage

Disadvantage

[4]

Total Marks ............... / 10

# Mechanical Systems 1

**1** State which type of motion is represented by each of the following descriptions.

**1.1)** Moving straight in one direction

........................................................................................................................................................... [1]

**1.2)** Moving backwards and forwards

........................................................................................................................................................... [1]

**1.3)** Moving in a circle

........................................................................................................................................................... [1]

**1.4)** Swinging backwards and forwards

........................................................................................................................................................... [1]

**2** **2.1)** State the type of lever shown below.

Load                    Effort

Not to scale

Fulcrum

........................................................................................................................................................... [1]

**2.2)** If the effort required to move a load of 185 N is 37 N, calculate the mechanical advantage of the lever.

...........................................................................................................................................................

...........................................................................................................................................................

...........................................................................................................................................................

........................................................................................................................................................... [2]

Total Marks ............... / 7

# Mechanical Systems 2

**1** Identify a type of linkage that could be used to carry out the following:

**1.1)** reverse the direction of a linear movement.

............................................................................................................................................................................ [1]

**1.2)** change the direction of motion by 90°.

............................................................................................................................................................................ [1]

**2** State how the following mechanisms change motion:

**2.1)** cam

............................................................................................................................................................................ [1]

**2.2)** worm gear

............................................................................................................................................................................ [1]

**2.3)** rack and pinion

............................................................................................................................................................................ [1]

**3** In a simple gear train, when the input gear rotates at a rate of 24 revolutions per minute (rpm) the output gear rotates at 108 rpm.

Calculate the gear ratio.

............................................................................................................................................................................

............................................................................................................................................................................

............................................................................................................................................................................

............................................................................................................................................................................ [2]

Total Marks ................ / 7

# Properties of Materials

**1** State the meaning of the following properties.

**1.1)** Hardness

.......................................................................................................................................................................

....................................................................................................................................................................... [1]

**1.2)** Fusibility

.......................................................................................................................................................................

....................................................................................................................................................................... [1]

**2** Complete the table, stating the term described by the first column.

An example has been completed for you.

| Description | Term | |
|---|---|---|
| *the ability of a material to not break when a force is applied to it suddenly* | *Toughness* | |
| the ability of a material to withstand a force or load that is applied to it | **2.1)** ............................. | [1] |
| the ability of a material to allow heat to pass through it | **2.2)** ............................. | [1] |
| the ability of a material to draw in moisture, light or heat | **2.3)** ............................. | [1] |

**3** Explain the difference between ductility and malleability.

.......................................................................................................................................................................

.......................................................................................................................................................................

.......................................................................................................................................................................

....................................................................................................................................................................... [2]

**Total Marks** .............. / 7

# Materials: Paper and Board

**1** State a typical application for each of the following types of paper and board.

| Type of Paper and Board | Typical Application | |
|---|---|---|
| Bleed-proof paper | 1.1) | [1] |
| Grid paper | 1.2) | [1] |
| Duplex board | 1.3) | [1] |
| Foil-lined board | 1.4) | [1] |
| Foam core board | 1.5) | [1] |

**2** Explain **two** reasons why manufacturers use corrugated cardboard to make boxes for packaging.

[4]

Total Marks _____ / 9

# Materials: Timber

**1** State **two** differences between softwood and hardwood.

1 ..............................................................................................................................................................

..............................................................................................................................................................

2 ..............................................................................................................................................................

..............................................................................................................................................................
[2]

**2** **2.1)** State **one** reason why natural timber may be seasoned before use.

..............................................................................................................................................................

..............................................................................................................................................................
[1]

**2.2)** Describe how timber is seasoned.

..............................................................................................................................................................

..............................................................................................................................................................

..............................................................................................................................................................

..............................................................................................................................................................
[2]

**3** Explain **two** advantages of manufactured boards over natural timbers.

..............................................................................................................................................................

..............................................................................................................................................................

..............................................................................................................................................................

..............................................................................................................................................................

..............................................................................................................................................................

..............................................................................................................................................................

..............................................................................................................................................................
[4]

Total Marks _____ / 9

# Materials: Metals

**1** Explain the difference between ferrous and non-ferrous metals.

[2]

**2** State a typical application for each of the following types of metal.

| Type of Metal | Typical Application | |
|---|---|---|
| High-carbon steel | **2.1)** | [1] |
| Copper | **2.2)** | [1] |
| Aluminium | **2.3)** | [1] |

**3** Describe the process involved in making metal from its raw material.

[4]

**Total Marks** ............... / 9

# Materials: Polymers

**1** For each of the polymers listed in the following table, state whether they are thermosetting or thermoforming, and list a typical application.

An example has been completed for you.

| Polymer | Thermosetting or Thermoforming | Typical Application |
|---|---|---|
| *Epoxy resin* | *Thermosetting* | *Printed circuit boards* |
| High-impact polystyrene (HIPS) | a) | b) |
| Melamine formaldehyde | c) | d) |
| Polymethyl-methacrylate (PMMA) | e) | f) |

[6]

**2** A manufacturer is producing water bottles from a polymer. Each bottle is made from 16 g of polymer. The manufacturer has 2.1 m³ of solid polymer, which has a density of 1400 kg m⁻³.

Calculate how many bottles the manufacturer could make. Assume that no material is wasted during the process.

......................................................................................................................................................

......................................................................................................................................................

......................................................................................................................................................

......................................................................................................................................................

......................................................................................................................................................

......................................................................................................................................................

...................................................................................................................................................... [4]

Total Marks .............. / 10

# Materials: Textiles

**1** Complete the table, identifying whether each fibre is natural or synthetic and giving a typical application.

An example has been completed for you.

| Fibre | Natural or Synthetic | Typical Application |
|---|---|---|
| *Cotton* | *Natural* | *Denim jeans* |
| Lycra | | |
| Wool | | |
| Nylon | | |
| Polyester | | |
| Silk | | |

[10]

**2** Explain why selvedge is important in woven fabrics.

......................................................................................................................................................

...................................................................................................................................................... [2]

Total Marks .................... / 12

# New Materials

**1** Complete the table, listing the 'smart' property of the listed materials and stating an application for which each material is typically used.

| Material | Smart Property | Typical Application |
|---|---|---|
| Thermochromic pigment | | |
| Photochromic pigment | | |
| Shape memory alloy | | |

[6]

**2** **2.1)** Explain the difference between a composite material and a metal alloy.

...................................................................................................................................

...................................................................................................................................

...................................................................................................................................

...................................................................................................................................

[2]

**2.2)** Name a composite material and give a typical application for which it is used.

...................................................................................................................................

...................................................................................................................................

...................................................................................................................................

...................................................................................................................................

[2]

Total Marks _____ / 10

# Standard Components

**1** Complete the table, naming a different standard component that is used with each material and stating what that component is used for.

An example has been completed for you.

| Material | Standard Component | Used for |
|---|---|---|
| *Metal* | *hinge* | *To attach the lid to a metal box* |
| Fabric | | |
| Timber | | |
| Paper | | |

[6]

**2** Explain why a company may decide to use standard components in a product.

........................................................................................................................................

........................................................................................................................................

........................................................................................................................................

........................................................................................................................................

........................................................................................................................................

........................................................................................................................................

........................................................................................................................................

[4]

Total Marks .............. / 10

# Finishing Materials

**1** Give **two** reasons why a finish may be applied to a material.

1 ...........................................................................................................................................

...........................................................................................................................................

2 ...........................................................................................................................................

........................................................................................................................................... **[2]**

**2** Describe the process of dip-coating a metal product.

...........................................................................................................................................

...........................................................................................................................................

...........................................................................................................................................

...........................................................................................................................................

...........................................................................................................................................

...........................................................................................................................................

...........................................................................................................................................

...........................................................................................................................................

........................................................................................................................................... **[5]**

**3** Name a finishing technique used with the following:

**3.1)** Wood

........................................................................................................................................... **[1]**

**3.2)** Printed circuit boards

........................................................................................................................................... **[1]**

Total Marks ............... / 9

# Selection of Materials

**1** Choose **one** of the following products by circling your selection:

Push-along toy for a small child          Swimsuit          Electrical system in a washing machine

Seating in a doctors' waiting room          Cooking pan

Discuss in detail the properties required by the product you have selected.

[9]

Total Marks ............ / 9

# Working with Materials

1 Explain **two** reasons why the design of a product may include features to provide reinforcement.

1 .................................................................................................................................................................

.................................................................................................................................................................

.................................................................................................................................................................

.................................................................................................................................................................

2 .................................................................................................................................................................

.................................................................................................................................................................

.................................................................................................................................................................

.................................................................................................................................................................

[4]

2 For each of the following materials, state one method used to change the properties of the material and the effect of that method on the properties.

An example has been completed for you.

| Material | How the Properties can be Modified | Effect |
|---|---|---|
| *Timber* | *Seasoning (drying)* | *Reduces risk of warping* |
| Aluminium | | |
| Polymers | | |
| Fabrics for furniture covers | | |

[6]

Total Marks _____ / 10

# Scales of Manufacture

**1** Select **one** of the following products:

An alarm circuit    A pair of curtains    Metal garden gates    Wooden wardrobes

A company currently manufactures the product you have selected for individual customers using one-off production. Due to interest from other customers, they are considering introducing batch manufacturing.

Discuss how this change could affect the manufacturing performance of the company.

[10]

**Total Marks** .............. / 10

# Manufacturing Processes 1: Process Types and Processes used with Paper and Board

Video Solution

Question 1

**1** Complete the table below, identifying a **different** tool or process that is typically used to carry out the tasks listed when using paper or card.

An example has been completed for you.

| Task | Tool |
|---|---|
| *Cutting or scoring card* | *Scissors* |
| Making a row of small holes in paper so that a part can be torn off easily | a) |
| Making straight cuts in large pieces of card | b) |
| Cutting out a complicated 2D net from card when a large quantity is needed | c) |
| Cutting a small circle in thin card | d) |
| Using a stencil and ink to apply a design to a one-off banner | e) |
| Printing large quantities of magazines using multiple colours | f) |

[6]

**2** **2.1)** Explain what is meant by 'laminating' a paper product.

......................................................................................................................................

......................................................................................................................................

......................................................................................................................................

......................................................................................................................................

[2]

**2.2)** Give an example of a laminated product that includes paper or card.

......................................................................................................................................

[1]

Total Marks _____ / 9

# Manufacturing Processes 2: Timber-Based Materials

**1** Identify **two** safety precautions that should be taken when using a wood lathe.

For each, give a reason why it is needed.

| Safety Precaution | Reason this is Needed |
|---|---|
| 1. | |
| 2. | |

[4]

**2** State **two** differences between a tenon saw and a coping saw.

1 ........................................................................................................................................

..........................................................................................................................................

2 ........................................................................................................................................

..........................................................................................................................................

[2]

**3** Describe how a curved product is made from natural timber by laminating.

..........................................................................................................................................

..........................................................................................................................................

..........................................................................................................................................

..........................................................................................................................................

..........................................................................................................................................

..........................................................................................................................................

..........................................................................................................................................

..........................................................................................................................................

..........................................................................................................................................

..........................................................................................................................................

[6]

Total Marks ............... / 12

# Manufacturing Processes 3: Metals and Alloys

**1** State **three** methods used to permanently join metal parts together.

1 ...........................................................................................................................................................

2 ...........................................................................................................................................................

3 ...........................................................................................................................................................  [3]

**2** Using notes and/or sketches, describe how a mould is made for sand casting.

[11]

Total Marks .................... / 14

# Manufacturing Processes 4: Polymers

**1** Label the features indicated by arrows on the injection moulding machine below.

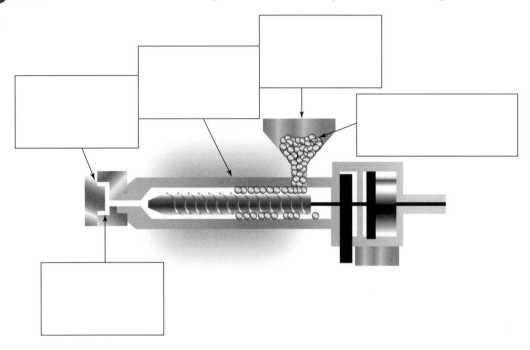

[5]

**2** State **two** methods that can be used to make a permanent joint in polymer products.

1 ........................................................................................................................................................

2 ........................................................................................................................................................  [2]

**3** Give **two** differences between the extrusion and injection moulding processes.

........................................................................................................................................................

........................................................................................................................................................

........................................................................................................................................................

........................................................................................................................................................

........................................................................................................................................................

........................................................................................................................................................

........................................................................................................................................................  [4]

Total Marks ................... / 11

# Manufacturing Processes 5: Textiles and Electronic Systems

1 State **two** techniques used to join different pieces of fabric together.

1 .........................................................................................................................................................

2 ..................................................................................................................................................... [2]

2 Explain what is meant by 'piping' on a textile product.

.........................................................................................................................................................

.........................................................................................................................................................

.........................................................................................................................................................

.........................................................................................................................................................

..................................................................................................................................................... [3]

3 State **two** methods used to make printed circuit boards (PCBs).

1 .........................................................................................................................................................

2 ..................................................................................................................................................... [2]

4 Explain **two** reasons why reflow (flow) soldering is used to make products in large quantities, rather than manual soldering.

.........................................................................................................................................................

.........................................................................................................................................................

.........................................................................................................................................................

.........................................................................................................................................................

.........................................................................................................................................................

.........................................................................................................................................................

..................................................................................................................................................... [6]

Total Marks .................... / 13

# Measurement and Production Aids

**1** State **one** reason why datum points are used when taking measurements.

_____

_____ [1]

**2** **2.1)** Describe the purpose of production aids.

_____

_____

_____

_____ [2]

**2.2)** Describe **two** different types of patterns that are used in Design and Technology applications.

1 _____

_____

2 _____

_____ [4]

**2.3)** Other than patterns, name **two** other types of production aids.

1 _____

2 _____ [2]

Total Marks _____ / 9

# Ensuring Accuracy

**1** State what is meant by the term 'precision'.

............................................................................................................................................

............................................................................................................................................

............................................................................................................................................ [1]

**2** Explain **two** ways that accuracy can be improved when manufacturing products.

1 ........................................................................................................................................

............................................................................................................................................

............................................................................................................................................

............................................................................................................................................

2 ........................................................................................................................................

............................................................................................................................................

............................................................................................................................................

............................................................................................................................................ [4]

**3** Explain the purpose of tolerances in manufacturing.

............................................................................................................................................

............................................................................................................................................

............................................................................................................................................

............................................................................................................................................ [2]

Total Marks ............... / 7

# Impact on Industry

1. State what is meant by the term 'planned obsolescence'.

[1

2. Give **three** benefits of a co-operative business model.

1

2

3

[3

3. Describe **two** examples of the use of automation in industrial product manufacture.

1

2

[4

Total Marks ............... / 8

# Impact on Production

**1** Describe **one** example of market pull and **one** example of technology push.

Market pull

................................................................................................................................

................................................................................................................................

................................................................................................................................

................................................................................................................................

Technology push

................................................................................................................................

................................................................................................................................

................................................................................................................................

................................................................................................................................ [4]

**2** **2.1)** Give **three** advantages of using CAD software over producing drawings by hand.

1 ..........................................................................................................................

................................................................................................................................

2 ..........................................................................................................................

................................................................................................................................

3 ..........................................................................................................................

................................................................................................................................ [3]

**2.2)** Explain **one** disadvantage of manufacturing products with CAM equipment over production using manual methods.

................................................................................................................................

................................................................................................................................

................................................................................................................................ [2]

Total Marks ............... / 9

# Impact on Society and the Environment

**1** Describe **two** examples of inclusive design.

1 _____

_____

_____

_____

2 _____

_____

_____

_____

[4]

**2** Describe, using an example, what is meant by a finite resource.

_____

_____

_____

_____

[2]

**3** State **two** examples of cultural issues that should be considered when designing products.

1 _____

_____

2 _____

_____

[2]

**Total Marks** _____ / 8

# Collins

## GCSE
# Design and Technology

Time allowed: 2 hours

## Materials

### For this paper you must have:

- writing and drawing instruments
- a calculator
- a protractor.

## Instructions

- Use black ink or black ball-point pen. Use pencils only for drawing.
- Answer **all** questions.
- Answer the questions in the spaces provided. Do not write on blank pages.
- Do all your work in this book. Cross through any work you do not want to be marked.

## Information

- The marks for questions are shown in brackets.
- The maximum mark for this paper is 100.
- There are 20 marks for Section A, 30 marks for Section B and 50 marks for Section C.

**Name:**

# Practice Exam Paper

## Section A

Questions **1–10** are multiple choice questions. You must shade in one lozenge.

**1**   Which one of the following sources of energy is a fossil fuel?

   **A**  biomass      ◯

   **B**  nuclear      ◯

   **C**  oil      ◯

   **D**  solar      ◯      **[1 mark]**

**2**   What does the term 'fusibility' describe?

   **A**  the ability of a material to burn   ◯

   **B**  the ability of a material to melt when heated   ◯

   **C**  the ability of a material to provide electrical resistance   ◯

   **D**  the ability of a material to be stretched without breaking   ◯   **[1 mark]**

3    Which one of the following is a ferrous metal?

**A**   aluminium    ◯

**B**   copper    ◯

**C**   tin    ◯

**D**   tool steel    ◯        **[1 mark]**

4    What type of motion is shown in Figure 1?

**Figure 1**

**A**   linear    ◯

**B**   oscillating    ◯

**C**   reciprocating    ◯

**D**   rotary    ◯        **[1 mark]**

5   Which one of the following is a synthetic fibre?

   **A**  cotton    ◯

   **B**  polyamide    ◯

   **C**  silk    ◯

   **D**  wool    ◯    **[1 mark]**

6   Which type of paper is commonly used for leaflets, as it resists inks and colours seeping through it?

   **A**  bleed-proof paper    ◯

   **B**  cartridge paper    ◯

   **C**  grid paper    ◯

   **D**  grid paper    ◯    **[1 mark]**

7   Which one of the following best describes market pull?

   **A**  advertising to increase the number of customers for a product    ◯

   **B**  prices for products being reduced over time    ◯

   **C**  products being produced due to new technologies becoming available    ◯

   **D**  the development of new products due to consumer demand    ◯    **[1 mark]**

**8** A designer is developing a system to automatically open a door when someone stands on a pressure sensor. What type of component is a pressure sensor?

A input ◯

B process ◯

C programmable ◯

D output ◯ **[1 mark]**

**9** A new product includes a removable cover so that the batteries can be replaced when they run out. This is an example of:

A anthropometric design ◯

B design for maintenance ◯

C flexible manufacturing ◯

D planned obsolescence ◯ **[1 mark]**

**1 0** Which one of the following is a softwood?

A balsa ◯

B mahogany ◯

C oak ◯

D pine ◯ **[1 mark]**

# Practice Exam Paper

**1 1 . 1** Figure 2 shows a simple gear train.

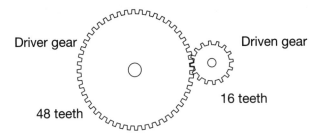

Driver gear    Driven gear

48 teeth    16 teeth

**Figure 2**

Calculate the gear ratio of this gear train.

[2 marks]

**1 1 . 2** Give **two** examples of a third-order lever.

1 .................................................................................................................................................................

2 .................................................................................................................................................................

[2 marks]

**1 2 . 1** Name a smart material.

.................................................................................................................................................................

[1 mark]

**1 2 · 2** For the material you have named in 12.1, state the property that makes it a smart material.

................................................................................................................................

................................................................................................................................

................................................................................................................................

**[1 mark]**

**1 3** Figure 3 shows a fork made from stainless steel.

**Figure 3**

State **two** reasons why forks are often made from stainless steel.

1 ............................................................................................................................

2 ............................................................................................................................

**[2 marks]**

**1 4** Describe briefly how electricity is generated using nuclear power.

................................................................................................................................

................................................................................................................................

................................................................................................................................

................................................................................................................................

................................................................................................................................

................................................................................................................................

**[2 marks]**

## Section B

1 5    Choose one product or component from Figure 4.

| Polymer chair | Mass-produced printed circuit board (PCB) | Card-based food packaging |
| --- | --- | --- |
| | | |
| Metal saw blade | Textile furniture covers | Wooden children's toy |
| | | |

**Figure 4**

Name of product: ...................................................................................

1 5 · 1 Explain how the material could be modified to improve one property or characteristic of this product.

........................................................................................................................

........................................................................................................................

........................................................................................................................

........................................................................................................................

........................................................................................................................

........................................................................................

........................................................................................

........................................................................................

**[4 marks]**

**1 5 · 2** For the product you have chosen, explain how **two** of the 6 Rs can be used to make the product more sustainable.

1 ........................................................................................

........................................................................................

........................................................................................

2 ........................................................................................

........................................................................................

........................................................................................

**[4 marks]**

**1 6** Describe the typical characteristics of the following types of production.

**1 6 · 1** Mass production

........................................................................................

........................................................................................

........................................................................................

........................................................................................

........................................................................................

........................................................................................

........................................................................................

**[3 marks]**

`1` `6` · `2` Batch production

.....................................................................................................................

.....................................................................................................................

.....................................................................................................................

.....................................................................................................................

.....................................................................................................................

**[2 marks]**

`1` `6` · `3` Prototype production

.....................................................................................................................

.....................................................................................................................

.....................................................................................................................

.....................................................................................................................

.....................................................................................................................

**[2 marks]**

`1` `7` Choose **one** of the products listed in Table 1.

| A monthly magazine | The wheel for a child's toy, made from wood | A block of metal with a milled slot | A template made from laser-cut polymer | Curtains with a printed repeating design | A printed circuit board (PCB) |
|---|---|---|---|---|---|

**Table 1**

Name of product/component: .........................................................................

`1` `7` · `1` Describe a quality control system that may be used during the manufacture of your chosen product.

.................................................................................................................................

.................................................................................................................................

.................................................................................................................................

.................................................................................................................................

.................................................................................................................................

.................................................................................................................................

.................................................................................................................................

.................................................................................................................................

**[3 marks]**

`1` `7` · `2` The part you have chosen has one feature with a dimension of 45 mm and a tolerance of 2 mm. Calculate the acceptable maximum and minimum sizes of the feature.

.................................................................................................................................

.................................................................................................................................

.................................................................................................................................

.................................................................................................................................

.................................................................................................................................

.................................................................................................................................

.................................................................................................................................

**[2 marks]**

1 8 Companies often consider social issues when designing and manufacturing products. These may include, for example, working conditions, pollution and the impact of the product and its manufacture on others.

Evaluate how the consideration of social issues may affect the design and manufacture of products.

Continue your answer on a separate piece of paper.

[10 marks]

# Section C

Figure 5 shows a mobile phone designed to help elderly people communicate with friends and family members.

**Figure 5**

Specification:

- Lightweight and portable
- Simple function – text messages and phone calls only
- Large buttons
- Battery powered

# Practice Exam Paper

1 9  Study the mobile phone and the information shown on the previous page.

1 9 · 1  Choose **two** of the specification points given. For each, explain why it was included.

Specification point 1: .............................................................................................................................

Explanation ..............................................................................................................................................

.....................................................................................................................................................................

.....................................................................................................................................................................

.....................................................................................................................................................................

Specification point 2: .............................................................................................................................

Explanation ..............................................................................................................................................

.....................................................................................................................................................................

.....................................................................................................................................................................

**[4 marks]**

1 9 · 2  Explain **one** improvement that would make the phone more suitable for the target audience.

.....................................................................................................................................................................

.....................................................................................................................................................................

.....................................................................................................................................................................

.....................................................................................................................................................................

.....................................................................................................................................................................

.....................................................................................................................................................................

.....................................................................................................................................................................

.....................................................................................................................................................................

**[3 marks]**

1 9 · 3 Explain how the design of the phone would need to be modified if the target audience was changed to teenagers.

........................................................................................................................................................

........................................................................................................................................................

........................................................................................................................................................

........................................................................................................................................................

........................................................................................................................................................

........................................................................................................................................................

........................................................................................................................................................

........................................................................................................................................................

........................................................................................................................................................

**[4 marks]**

2 0  The mobile phone shown on page 213 is powered by a battery. The company collected data on how long the batteries lasted before they needed replacing, see Table 2. Data was recorded for 50 products.

No battery needed replacing in less than 50 hours. All of the batteries needed replacing in less than 150 hours.

| Battery life, hours | 50 < 70 | 70 < 90 | 90 < 110 | 110 < 130 | 130 < 150 |
|---|---|---|---|---|---|
| Cumulative total number of failed batteries | 1 | 5 | 14 | 30 | 50 |

**Table 2**

2 0 · 1  Produce a line graph of the cumulative battery life.

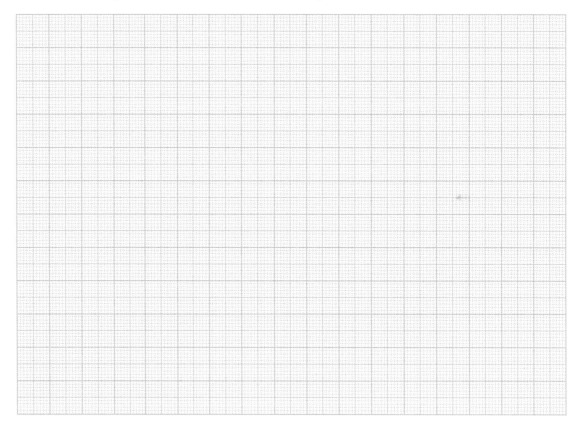

[5 marks]

**2 0** · **2** Calculate the mean average number of hours for the life of the batteries.

**[2 marks]**

**2 0** · **3** Determine the time at which 50% of the batteries needed to be replaced.

**[2 marks]**

**2 0** · **4** Explain the difference between the values calculated in 20.2 and 20.3.

**[2 marks]**

# Practice Exam Paper

2 1 User-centred design was applied during the design of the phone shown on page 213.

2 1 · 1 Explain **two** advantages of user-centred design as a design strategy.

1 ........................................................................................................................................

........................................................................................................................................

........................................................................................................................................

........................................................................................................................................

........................................................................................................................................

2 ........................................................................................................................................

........................................................................................................................................

........................................................................................................................................

........................................................................................................................................

........................................................................................................................................

**[4 marks]**

2 1 · 2 State **two** disadvantages of user-centred design as a design strategy.

1 ........................................................................................................................................

........................................................................................................................................

........................................................................................................................................

2 ........................................................................................................................................

........................................................................................................................................

**[2 marks]**

**2 1 · 3** Another example of a design strategy used in the design of the mobile phone is the systems approach.

Explain what is meant by the systems approach.

......................................................................................................................................................

......................................................................................................................................................

......................................................................................................................................................

**[2 marks]**

**2 2** Figure 6 shows a shape that is to be marked out for cutting.

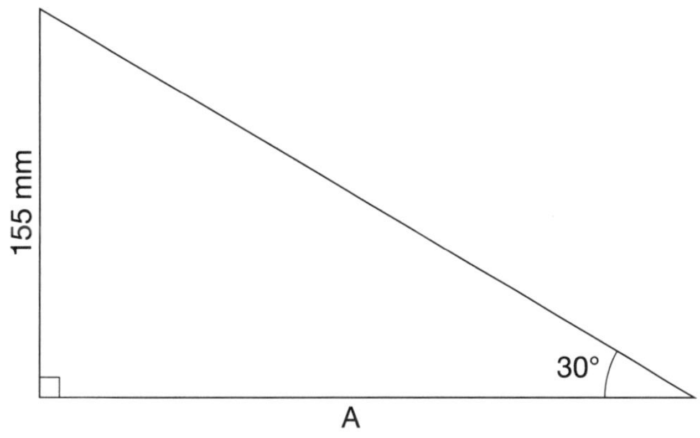

**Figure 6**

Not to scale

**2 2 · 1** Calculate the length of side A. Give your answer to one decimal place.

......................................................................................................................................................

......................................................................................................................................................

......................................................................................................................................................

......................................................................................................................................................

......................................................................................................................................................

**[2 marks]**

# Practice Exam Paper

2 2 · 2 Explain the purpose of datums when marking out materials.

.......................................................................................................................................

.......................................................................................................................................

.......................................................................................................................................

.......................................................................................................................................

**[2 marks]**

2 2 · 3 Give **two** methods of reducing waste when cutting or shaping materials.

1 ....................................................................................................................................

.......................................................................................................................................

2 ....................................................................................................................................

.......................................................................................................................................

**[2 marks]**

2 3 · 1 Give **two** examples of surface treatments or finishes.

1 ....................................................................................................................................

.......................................................................................................................................

2 ....................................................................................................................................

.......................................................................................................................................

**[2 marks]**

2 3 · 2 Give **two** reasons why surface treatments or finishes are applied to materials.

1 ....................................................................................................................................

.......................................................................................................................................

2 ....................................................................................................................................

.......................................................................................................................................

**[2 marks]**

2 3 · 3 For one of your examples given in question **23.1**, use notes and sketches to describe how this surface treatment or finish would be applied to a material.

[5 marks]

# Practice Exam Paper

**2 4** · **1** Explain what is meant by 'design fixation'.

......................................................................................................................................

......................................................................................................................................

**[2 marks]**

**2 4** · **2** Explain why designers produce prototypes of products or systems.

......................................................................................................................................

......................................................................................................................................

**[3 marks]**

**END OF QUESTIONS**

# Answers

## Page 164 Design Strategies

1.  1 mark for each suitable response. For example:

| Design Approach | Advantage of Strategy | Disadvantage of Strategy |
|---|---|---|
| Iterative design | Problems with the design can be discovered and dealt with earlier [1]. | It can be time consuming if a lot of prototypes or iterations need to be produced [1]. |
| User-centred design | The end user has a greater ownership of the final product [1]. | The design could become too focused on one particular end user's requirements [1]. |
| Systems thinking | It is easier to find errors or faults in the design [1]. | It can lead to the use of components that are not necessary [1]. |

## Page 165 Electronic Systems

1.  1 mark for stating whether each component is an input, process or output and 1 mark for suitable application of each. For example:

| Component | Input, Process or Output | Application |
|---|---|---|
| Push switch | Input [1] | Starting the timing sequence on a kitchen timer [1] |
| Lamp | Output [1] | Providing light for a bicycle safety light [1] |
| Microcontroller | Process [1] | Controlling the counting sequence for the score counter on a board game [1] |
| Thermistor | Input [1] | Temperature sensor for an automatic heating system [1] |
| Buzzer | Output [1] | Making a buzzing sound for a doorbell [1] |

## Page 166 The Work of Others: Designers

1.  1 mark for any suitable designer from the specification. For example: Coco Chanel [1].
2.  1 mark for a product designed by the designer given in answer to question 1. For example: Chanel suit [1].
3.  1 mark for each suitable feature of the design given in answer to question 2. For example: Chanel suit: masculine/bold look [1], three-piece sleeve [1], machine-quilted lining on jacket [1], made with soft/flexible materials [1].

## Page 167 The Work of Others: Companies

1.  1 mark for any suitable design company from the specification. For example: Under Armour [1].
2.  1 mark for a product designed by the company given in answer to question 1. For example: moisture-wicking t-shirt [1].
3.  1 mark for each suitable feature of the design given in answer to question 2. For example: moisture-wicking t-shirt: keeps athlete cool [1], removes sweat from body [1], lightweight [1], made using microfibres [1].

## Page 168 Ecological, Environmental and Social Issues

1.  Up to 2 marks for explanation of each way. For example: choose recyclable materials [1] so that less new material needs to be sourced [1]. Design for disassembly [1] so that materials/components can be reused [1]. Select a sustainable power supply [1] to reduce reliance on non-renewable energy [1].
2.  Up to 2 marks for definition. For example: fair trade is a movement that works to help people in developing countries [1] get a fair deal for the products that they produce [1].

## Page 169 Research and Investigation

1.  Up to 2 marks for explanation. For example: to find out if there is a gap in the market [1] so that a product will be commercially successful [1].
2.  Up to 2 marks for explanation. For example: to gain feedback from potential customers [1] to ensure that the product will meet their needs [1].
3.  1 mark for each correct type of data. For example: primary data [1]; secondary data [1].
4.  1 mark for correct answer: b

## Page 170 Briefs and Specifications

1.  1 mark for each specification point and 1 mark for explanation for each. Specification may relate to any suitable product that matches the brief. For example:
    - The product must use bright and attractive colours [1] so it would appeal aesthetically to the child [1].
    - The product must have no sharp edges [1] so as not to cause injury to the child [1].
    - The product must have a set of lettered blocks [1] so that the child can practise making different words [1].

## Page 171 Exploring and Developing Ideas

1.  1 mark for each suitable stage given. For example: modelling [1], testing [1], evaluating [1], improving/refining outcome [1].
2.  1 mark for each reason or 2 marks for each reason explained further, up to a maximum of 4 marks. For example: to get ideas onto paper very quickly [1] as freehand sketches do not have to follow drawing conventions [1]. To share early ideas with clients [1] so that they can provide feedback [1].

## Page 172 Communication of Ideas 1

1.  To show how the parts of a product fit together [1]
2.  2.1) Award 1 mark for each of the following:
    - Design appears to be in correct proportion/to scale.
    - Vertical lines/leading edges go straight up.
    - Correct use of guidelines for the horizontal lines.
    - Design is clearly visible as some form of mobile phone stand.
    2.2) Award marks up to a maximum of 4 marks as follows:
    - 1 mark each for two materials or one material and one finish; or 2 marks for a material with an explanation of why it is suggested.
    - 1 mark each for two identified manufacturing processes; or 2 marks for a manufacturing process with an explanation of why it is suggested.

## Page 173 Communication of Ideas 2

1.  Award 1 mark for each of the following, up to a maximum of 12 marks:
    - labels showing the input [1], process [1], output [1] and at least one of the signals [1]
    - sensor as the input
    - timer as the process block
    - siren as the output block
    - movement as the input signal
    - sound as the output signal

- electricity as the signal between the input and process
- electricity as the signal between the process and output
- all parts in the correct orientation.

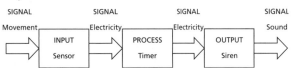

2. To give an impression of the size/shape of the product [1] at lower cost than using the actual parts to make the prototype [1] OR because it is much quicker to make a card model [1] than to obtain the materials and build a prototype from them [1].

## Page 174 Computer-Based Tools

1. c [1]
2. a [1]
3. Any 4 from: to create a bill of materials [1], to create a virtual model of a design [1], to virtually test a design [1], to create a rapid prototype [1], to programme/send instructions to CAM equipment [1], to create images to present to a client [1].

## Page 175 Prototype Development

1. 1 mark each for any four of the following: to check how a product will function [1]; to check how a product will look [1]; to present to a client to get their feedback [1]; to ensure that problems with a product are found before starting manufacture [1]; to determine if it can be produced at the required cost [1].
2. Prototypes are typically made as one-off products [1] whereas the final products may be made in large quantities [1]. Prototypes may be made from a different material [1] or use different manufacturing processes [1] due to the small quantity being made [1], so may not necessarily have identical properties to the final product produced in quantity [1].

## Page 176 Energy Generation and Storage

1. 1 mark for stating whether each source of energy is renewable or non-renewable and up to 2 marks for suitable description of how each is used to produce energy. For example:

| Source of Energy | Renewable or Non-Renewable | Description of How Energy is Produced |
|---|---|---|
| Tidal | Renewable [1] | Tidal flow turns turbines [1] which then drive generators to produce electricity [1]. |
| Coal | Non-renewable [1] | Coal is burnt [1] and the heat is used to create steam [1] which is used to drive generators to produce electricity [1]. |

2. Award 1 mark for stating an advantage and 1 mark for a disadvantage, with a further mark for each supporting explanation up to a maximum of 4 marks. Advantages could include: uninterrupted supply of energy [1] as power is produced 24/7 [1]; less reliance upon fossil fuels [1] resulting in less production of carbon dioxide/global warming [1]. Disadvantages could include: risk of pollution [1] due to toxic nature of materials used/waste produced [1]; risk of health issues [1] if workers are directly subjected to radiation [1]; uses uranium [1] which is a non-renewable resource [1].

## Page 177 Mechanical Systems 1

1. 1.1) Linear [1]
   1.2) Reciprocating [1]
   1.3) Rotating [1]
   1.4) Oscillating [1]
2. 2.1) Second-order [1]
   2.2) Mechanical advantage = load / effort [1] = 185 / 37 = 5 [1]

## Page 178 Mechanical Systems 2

1. 1.1) push-pull linkage [1]
   1.2) bell crank [1]
2. 2.1) converts rotary motion to reciprocating motion [1].
   2.2) changes rotary motion through 90° [1].
   2.3) changes rotary motion into linear motion [1].
3. Gear ratio = speed of output gear / speed of input gear [1] = 108 / 24 = 4.5:1 = 9:2 [1]

## Page 179 Properties of Materials

1. 1.1) The ability of a material to resist wear or being scratched [1]
   1.2) The ability of a material to be changed from a solid to a liquid by heat [1]
2. 2.1) Strength [1]
   2.2) Thermal conductivity [1]
   2.3) Absorbency [1]
3. Ductility is the measurable amount that a material can be stretched or deformed by an applied force [1] whereas malleability is the ability for the shape to be changed without breaking, which may occur progressively with a much lower force [1].

## Page 180 Materials: Paper and Board

1. 1.1) E.g. printed multi-coloured flyers and leaflets [1]
   1.2) E.g. quick sketches and model making [1]
   1.3) E.g. food packaging [1]
   1.4) E.g. drinks cartons or ready meal lids [1]
   1.5) E.g. architectural models [1]
2. Award up to 4 marks for any of the following: It is lighter than solid material [1] because it is made of two layers with an interlacing fluted section [1] so will be easier to carry or transport [1]. It is often made from recycled materials [1] so is more environmentally friendly than other types of board [1]. Strength-for-weight [1] it is cheaper than solid board [1].

## Page 181 Materials: Timber

1. Softwood trees keep their foliage all year, whereas hardwood trees lose their leaves in the autumn [1]. This means that softwood grows faster than hardwood [1].
2. 2.1) To make it less likely to warp/distort [1]
   2.2) Award 1 mark for the first point and 1 mark for either the second OR third point: It is dried [1], either slowly in air [1] or by gentle heating in a large kiln [1].
3. Up to 4 marks for any of the following: The properties of manufactured boards are typically uniform [1] as they do not have a grain [1]. Manufactured boards are available in large sheets [1] whereas the size of natural timber planks is limited by the size of the tree [1]. Manufactured boards can be more environmentally friendly [1] as they can be made from offcuts or recycled material [1].

## Page 182 Materials: Metals

1. Ferrous metals contain iron [1]; non-ferrous metals do not contain iron [1].
2. 2.1) Award 1 mark for a suitable response, e.g. Tools or springs [1]
   2.2) Electrical wiring [1] or water pipes [1]
   2.3) Drinks cans [1] or cooking pans [1]
3. Award up to 4 marks for any of the following: Metal ore [1] is extracted from the ground by mining or quarrying [1]. This is refined by heating it [1], by using chemical reactions to remove unwanted elements [1] or by electrolysis [1]. After refining, metals are typically melted [1] and either cast into products or shaped into stock forms [1].

## Page 183 Materials: Polymers

1. a) Thermoforming [1]
   b) E.g. Packaging [1]
   c) Thermosetting [1]

d) E.g. Laminates for kitchen worktops [1]
e) Thermoforming [1]
f) E.g. Display signs [1]
2. Weight of polymer available = 2.1 × 1.4 [1] = 2940 kg [1]
Number of bottles = 2940 / 0.016 [1] = 183,750 bottles [1]

## Page 184 Materials: Textiles

1. 1 mark for each correctly completed cell

| Fibre | Natural or Synthetic | Typical Application |
|-------|----------------------|---------------------|
| Cotton | Natural | Denim jeans |
| Lycra | Synthetic | E.g. Sportswear, underwear, socks, suits |
| Wool | Natural | E.g. Felt, flannel, gabardine; jumpers, suits, dresses, carpets |
| Nylon | Synthetic | E.g. Tights and stockings, sportswear, upholstery, carpets |
| Polyester | Synthetic | E.g. Sportswear |
| Silk | Natural | E.g. Chiffon, organza, crepe, velvet; dresses, shirts, ties |

2. Selvedge is an edge that will not fray [1]; it is important as otherwise the fabric will start to unravel and fray when cut [1].

## Page 185 New Materials

1. 1 mark for each correctly completed cell

| Material | Smart Property | Typical Application |
|----------|----------------|---------------------|
| Thermochromic pigment | Changes colour in response to temperature | E.g. flexible thermometers, food packaging |
| Photochromic pigment | Becomes darker / changes colour in response to increased brightness | E.g. sunglasses |
| Shape memory alloy | Reverts to its original shape when heat is applied | E.g. spectacle frames, fire detectors |

2. 2.1) Composites combine the properties of two or more materials [1]. Unlike an alloy, the materials in a composite are not mixed at a chemical level / can be seen to be separate within the structure when looking at the material under a microscope [1].
2.2) Award 1 mark for a material and 1 mark for an application. For example, glass-reinforced polyester (GRP)/fibreglass [1], used in car body building and repair of boat hulls [1]; carbon-reinforced polyester (CRP) [1], used to make tent poles/high-performance bicycles/sports equipment [1].

## Page 186 Standard Components

1. 1 mark for each correctly completed cell

| Material | Standard Component | Used For |
|----------|--------------------|----------|
| Metal | hinge | To attach the lid to a metal box |
| Fabric | E.g. zip, press studs, velcro, buttons and poppers, decorative items | To fasten two sides of a garment together |
| Timber | E.g. woodscrews, hinges, knockdown fittings | To attach the sides to a wooden box |
| Paper | E.g. binders, clips, fasteners | To hold the pages of a document together |

2. Award marks as indicated, up to a maximum of 4 marks. For example: making components in small quantities can be very expensive [1] due to the labour time [1] and equipment required [1]. It normally costs less to buy standard components [1] and they can offer more consistent quality [1]. Any other relevant point.

## Page 187 Finishing Materials

1. Any 2 of: To improve aesthetics [1] or corrosion resistance [1], to allow a lower cost material to be used for a product [1], to improve functionality [1].
2. Air is blown through a polymer powder [1] to make it behave like a liquid [1]. The metal product is heated [1] then dipped into the fluidised powder [1], which melts and sticks to the surface [1].
3. 3.1) Painting / varnishing / tanalising [1]
   3.2) Laquering [1]

## Page 188 Selection of Materials

1. 7–9 marks: thorough knowledge and understanding of the properties required, with a minimum of four properties considered. Explanations are given for why all the identified properties are needed. 4–6 marks: good knowledge and understanding of the properties required, with a minimum of three properties considered. Explanation included for why some of the identified properties are needed. 1–3 marks: limited knowledge or understanding. Mainly descriptive response, stating a few of the properties required.

Properties specific to the application that could be considered include the following.

| Push-along toy for a small child | • Toughness, to resist impacts<br>• Non-toxic, so it doesn't harm the child if put in mouth<br>• Malleability, ability to be made into the shape of the toy<br>• Hardness, to resist being scratched or damaged in use |
|---|---|
| Cooking pan | • Ability to conduct heat from the hob<br>• Corrosion resistance so that it isn't damaged by the food that it makes contact with during use.<br>• Non-toxic, so it doesn't taint the food<br>• Toughness, to resist impact if hit or dropped<br>• Malleability, ability to be made into the shape of the pan |
| Swimsuit | • Absorbency, to prevent spoilage of contents or damage to the packaging<br>• Ability to be printed on, to give aesthetic appeal<br>• Corrosion resistance – to not be damaged by the water or sunlight. |
| Seating in a doctors' waiting room | • Aesthetics – colour and texture that appeal to the user<br>• Ease of cleaning<br>• Hardwearing so it lasts a long time<br>• Non-flammable, so that it doesn't burn |
| Electrical system in a washing machine | • Electrical conductivity – it should insulate the circuitry to prevent electric shocks to the user<br>• Resistance to corrosion, so that it isn't damaged by the washing powder or water when in use<br>• Strength, to support the weight of the water |

In addition, general properties (in addition to the above list, where not duplicated) could include: functionality, aesthetics, environmental considerations, availability of materials, cost, social factors, quality, user (e.g. sizes, weights), ethical considerations and cultural factors.

# Page 189 Working with Materials

1. Award 1 mark for each reason with a second mark for each explanation up to a maximum of 4 marks: To achieve the properties needed in an application [1] whilst using the minimum amount of material [1]. It costs less to reinforce just the area where enhanced properties are needed [1], rather than using a more expensive material with superior properties [1] The product would weigh less [1] than if a thicker material was used for the whole design [1].

2. Award 1 mark for each correct cell:

| Material | How the Properties can be Modified | Effect |
|---|---|---|
| Timber | Seasoning (drying) | Reduces risk of warping |
| Aluminium | E.g. Annealing or Anodizing | E.g. increases malleability or increases surface hardness |
| Polymers | Adding stabilisers | Prevents degradation by UV light |
| Fabrics for furniture covers | Adding flame retardants | Reduces fire hazards |

# Page 190 Scales of Manufacture

1. Award up to 10 marks as follows: Changing from one off production to batch production could reduce the cost per product [1] as slightly less labour time will be required per product [1]. The skill level needed by the workers may not need to be as high [1] as one-off manufacture is typically carried out by highly skilled workers [1], which may mean that the labour cost per hour can be reduced [1].
Batch production groups identical products together which means that there is less non-making time due to equipment changeovers [1].
In one-off production the workers ensure high quality by checking every product [1] whereas in batch manufacturing, the company may choose to check samples from batches [1] thus reducing inspection costs [1].
In batch manufacture, each item in the batch will be the same [1] whereas in one-off manufacture, changes can more easily be made to suit the needs of individual customers [1].
Dedicated jigs may be used to speed up some processes [1]. Some processes may be automated, speeding up production [1]; the cost of equipment needed for automation can be divided between the quantity of products made [1].
Customers may be unhappy/place fewer orders [1] as they may want unique or custom items that other people do not have [1]. Any other relevant point.

# Page 191 Manufacturing Processes 1: Process Types and Processes used with Paper and Board

1. a) perforation cutter [1]
   b) guillotine or rotary cutter [1]
   c) die cutter [1]
   d) compass cutter, circle cutter or craft knife/scalpel [1]
   e) screen printing [1]
   f) offset lithography [1]
2. 2.1) Award 1 mark each for any two of the following: Adding layers of material [1] which may be of a different material (polymer/metal) [1] using heat or adhesive [1] which creates a composite [1]
   2.2) E.g. Takeaway food containers [1]

# Page 192 Manufacturing Processes 2: Timber-Based Materials

1. Award 1 mark for each safety precaution and 1 mark for each reason it is needed up to a maximum of 4 marks. E.g. eye goggles/face screen [1] to protect against swarf/flying debris [1]; tying back loose clothing/long hair [1] to protect against entanglement in the rotating chuck [1]; machine guard [1] to protect against any part that is ejected in use [1].
2. Award 1 mark each for any two of the following: A tenon saw has a rigid/reinforced blade where the coping saw has a narrow thin blade [1]. Tenon saws are used to make straight cuts in wood whereas coping saws are used to make curved cuts in thin sheet [1]. Tenon saws are used just with wood whereas coping saws can be used with thin sheets of wood or polymer [1]
3. A former is made [1]. Thin sheets/plies of the timber [1] are glued together using PVA [1]. These are shaped round the former while the glue is wet [1] and clamped in place until the glue dries [1] when it will retain the shape of the former [1].

# Page 193 Manufacturing Processes 3: Metals and Alloys

1. Welding [1], brazing [1], epoxy resin adhesive [1]
2. Make a pattern in two halves [1]
Place the patten in the drag [1] and cover with oil-bonded sand [1].
Apply pressure to make sure the sand is pushed into all features [1].
Turn the drag upside down [1] and carefully place on the other half of the pattern [1].
Put in place sprue pins [1] to create runners and risers [1].
Cover the cope with oil-bonded sand, ensuring sand is pushed into all the features [1].
Take apart the drag and cope and carefully remove the pattern and sprues [1]
Re-assemble the mould ready for use [1].

# Page 194 Manufacturing Processes 4: Polymers

1. Award 1 mark for each correctly identified feature.

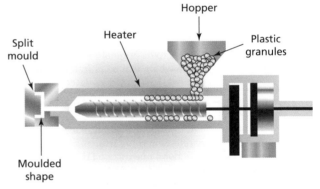

2. Solvent cement/adhesive [1], welding [1]
3. Extrusion uses a die [1] where injection moulding uses a mould [1];
Extrusion can only make continuous products (such as tubes or sections) [1] where injection moulding can make complex three-dimensional products [1].

# Page 195 Manufacturing Processes 5: Textiles and Electronic Systems

1. Sewing [1], bonding [1]
2. It is a type of trim [1] made from a strip of folded fabric inserted in a seam [1] to define an edge/style line [1]
3. Any two of: silk screen printing [1], photoengraving [1], milling [1].
4. In manual soldering, components are pushed through the circuit board [1] whereas in flow soldering, components are mounted on top of the circuit board [1] which is easier to locate [1]. In manual soldering, solder is applied to each joint individually [1] whereas in flow soldering, the whole assembly is heated, making all the joints in one go [1], meaning that it is much quicker for a complicated circuit board [1].

### Page 196 Measurement and Production Aids

1. To provide reference points for the measurements [1]
2. 2.1) To provide accuracy [1] and precision of production [1].
   2.2) Textile/fabric patterns [1] which are used to trace parts of a garment onto fabric before it is cut [1]. Casting patterns for metal/plastic resin [1] which are used to prepare a cavity for pouring in the molten material [1].
   2.3) Jigs [1], templates [1]

### Page 197 Ensuring Accuracy

1. How repeatable/reproducible a measurement is [1].
2. Increased use of CAD/CAM equipment [1] as computerised equipment is more accurate than human operators [1]. Use of jigs/templates [1] as these can be used to hold a material/guide cutting tools [1].
3. To give the permissible level of variation in the dimensions of a manufactured product [1] so that issues such as improper fits/wasted materials/non-functioning products are avoided [1].

### Page 198 Impact on Industry

1. A business strategy where a product is designed to be no longer useful after a set period of time [1].
2. Can be set up by just a small number of people [1], benefits from buying power of whole membership [1], all members share in the profits made [1].
3. Award 1 mark each for up to four of the following points: Use of automated robotic arms [1] for assembling products on a production line [1]. Use of automated sensor systems [1] for detecting defects in manufactured products [1]. Use of CAM/CNC equipment [1] for cutting materials to shape/size [1].

### Page 199 Impact on Production

1. Market pull: The development of the digital camera [1] which has become smaller/lighter/better performing as a result of customer wants/needs [1].
   Technology push: Smartphones/tablet computers [1] which were developed as a result of improvements in touch screen technology [1].
2. 2.1) Award 1 mark each for up to three of the following points: Greater accuracy [1], ease of modification [1], reduced storage requirements [1], ease of sharing digitally [1], can be exported to CAM/CNC equipment [1], drawings can be automatically produced from 3D models [1], designs can be simulated [1].
   2.2) High setup costs [1] which can be prohibitive to businesses with small turnovers/manufacturing quotas [1].

### Page 200 Impact on Society and the Environment

1. Award 1 mark each for up to two of the following points: A phone with large buttons [1] designed for use by elderly people [1]. A garden tool with an ergonomic handle [1] for people who suffer from arthritis [1]. A door with a handle that can be pulled from different heights [1] that can be used by people in wheelchairs and/or children as well as adults [1].
2. A resource that will eventually run out [1], for example fossil fuels/metals/oil-based plastics/woods from trees that are not replaced [1].
3. Award 1 mark each for up to two of the following points: Religious preferences/faiths/beliefs [1], current trends [1], use/meaning of colour [1], use/meaning of language [1], different meanings of logos/symbols [1].

### Pages 202–207 Practice Exam Paper Section A

1. C [1]
2. B [1]
3. D [1]
4. B [1]
5. B [1]
6. A [1]
7. D [1]
8. A [1]
9. B [1]
10. D [1]
11. 11.1) Gear ratio = number of teeth on driven gear / number of teeth on driver gear. Gear ratio = 16:48 [1]
    Reducing to lowest common denominator, Gear ratio = 1:3 [1]
    Note: this must be presented as a ratio. The answer mark will not be awarded for a decimal value, i.e. 0.33.
    11.2) 1 mark each for two suitable examples, for example: a broom, a fishing rod, a pair of tweezers, a spade/shovel, a hammer.
12. 12.1) 1 mark each for two suitable examples, for example: shape memory alloys, thermochromic pigments, photochromic pigments.
    12.2) 1 mark for stating the smart property of the material named in 12.1, for example: returns to original shape when heated, changes colour with temperature, changes colour with changes in the level of light, respectively.
13. 1 mark each for two suitable reasons. For example: resistant to corrosion, non-toxic/will not taint food, can be reused, strength/doesn't bend when used, can be placed in a dishwasher. Any other appropriate answer.
14. The nuclear pile generates heat/turns water into steam [1]. The steam turns a generator, producing electricity [1].

### Pages 208–212 Practice Exam Paper Section B

15. 15.1) 1 mark for identifying the property modified, 1 mark for stating how it could be modified and up to 2 marks for detail about the modification or reasons why it is modified. For example, polymer chair – improved durability [1] by adding stabilisers to resist UV degradation [1] as this stops sunshine weakening the polymer [1] as it is used outside [1]. Mass-produced PCB – minimising cost [1] by the use of photosensitive board [1] to enable rapid production [1] of complex designs [1]. Card-based food packaging – reduced absorbency [1] by the use of additives to prevent moisture transfer [1] so that the packaging does not become soggy [1] when it contains hot food that gives off moisture [1]. Metal saw blade – heat treatment [1] to prevent brittleness of the blade [1] whilst keeping a hard cutting edge [1], enabling a lower cost material to be used [1]. Textile furniture covers – reduce flammability [1] by treating with flame retardants [1] to minimise risk of home fires [1] if it is accidentally set alight by a cigarette or electrical spark [1]. Wooden children's toy – improved dimensional stability [1] by seasoning [1] to reduce the moisture content [1] in case the wood is stored outside in the rain [1]. Note: the use of different surface finishes with appropriate detail and reasons will also be awarded marks.
    15.2) 1 mark each for stating two of the 6 Rs and 1 mark each for explaining how the chosen product could be modified and the implications of this modification. For example, reuse [1] – such as giving the wooden toy to a different child when the initial child grows older and loses interest in it [1]. Recycle [1] – such as melting down old saw blades so that they can be used in new products [1]. Rethink [1] – such as creating multi-use packaging rather than disposable food packaging [1]. Reduce [1] – such as making textile furniture covers that only cover the visible parts of the furniture (i.e. not the back) [1]. Refuse [1] – such as buying chairs made from sustainable material rather than polymers [1]. Repair [1] – such as using standard parts on the PCB to allow replacements when it fails [1].
16. 16.1) Up to 3 marks for details such as: very large number of products produced [1] often using a production line [1]. This can involve high use of CAM (computer-aided manufacture) equipment [1] and sub-assemblies [1].

**16.2)** Up to 2 marks for details such as: fixed quantity of identical products manufactured [1]; jigs and templates often used to aid production [1]; flexible machines that can be changed over to produce different products [1].

**16.3)** Up to 2 marks for details such as: manufacture of a bespoke single item [1] typically by highly skilled workers [1]; flexible machines that may be manually controlled [1].

**17. 17.1)** Award up to 3 marks for identifying an appropriate quality control system and giving details about its implementation. For example, monthly magazine – use of registration marks [1]. These are printed outside the trim area of printing [1] and allow the printer to accurately align separate press plates for multi-colour print jobs [1]. Wooden wheel – go/no-go gauge [1]. If the wheel fits between the maximum indicators, it is less than the maximum tolerance [1]; if it does not fit between the markers for the minimum size, it is above the minimum tolerance [1]. Slotted metal block – using a depth-stop [1] pre-set to the required depth [1] with machining stopping when the depth-stop contacts the material [1]. Polymer template – selecting the correct laser settings [1], such as % power [1] and cutting speed [1]. Curtains – using an original sample/master [1] to check the dimensions of the repeat print [1] and its colour [1]. PCB – controlling times for UV exposure [1], developing [1] and etching [1].

**17.2)** 43 mm [1] and 47 mm [1]

**18.** 9–10 marks: excellent understanding shown and points well evaluated in depth. Appropriate and fully justified conclusions presented. 7–8 marks: good understanding shown and points well evaluated. Appropriate conclusions presented with some justification. 5–6 marks: good understanding shown with some points evaluated. Appropriate but unjustified conclusions presented. 3–4 marks: some understanding shown. Limited evaluation. Limited conclusions made. 1–2 marks: few points made or one point made with some limited explanation. No conclusion. 0 marks: no response worthy of merit. Indicative content: use the following as points for further evaluation to demonstrate understanding. If other valid responses are presented, they should also be given full credit. Working conditions – conformance of factories to safety legislation and standards; legal and ethical implications of non-compliance; how conformance may vary between countries; effect on the manufacturing cost. Pollution – impact on marine/local habitats; potential for contamination of the food chain; potential options for reducing pollution and how these may affect the design and manufacture of products; disposal of products at the end of their life. Impacts on others – potential negative impacts; consideration of social footprint, ethical issues and the materials used in products; influence on the wider society. Whilst candidates can answer in general terms, responses may include specific examples of products – credit will be awarded if these are appropriate.

## Pages 213–222 Practice Exam Paper Section C

**19. 19.1)** 1 mark for each relevant point of explanation, up to maximum of 2 marks per specification point chosen. For example, simple function – no unnecessary features [1], making it easier for someone not confident with technology to use the phone [1]. Large buttons – easier for elderly people to see the buttons/numbers [1] so suitable for users with poor eyesight [1]; easier to press [1] so suitable for people with arthritis, etc. [1].

**19.2)** 1 mark for identifying a relevant improvement and up to 2 marks for explaining how it would make the phone more suitable. For example, the phone could be given a more ergonomic shape [1]. This would make it easier to grip [1] and therefore reduce fatigue during use [1].

**19.3)** 1 mark for each suitable point relating to colour, shape, screen size/type, features of the phone, etc. up to a maximum of 4 marks. For example, including additional features on the phone such as multiple cameras [1] and WiFi access [1]. Increasing the memory [1] so that it can hold apps [1]. Making it a brighter colour [1] so that it is more attractive to teenage buyers [1]. Including a larger screen [1] so that they can see more detail when running apps or looking at social media [1]. Having touch-sensitive capability [1] to allow data input or selection of options [1].

**20. 20.1)** 1 mark for making the battery life the $x$ axis and the total number of failed batteries the $y$ axis; 1 mark for appropriate range of values for the axes; 1 mark for a line starting at 50,0; 1 mark for points plotted at the top end of each band (70, 90, 110, 130, 150); 1 mark for a line approximating to the correct shape.

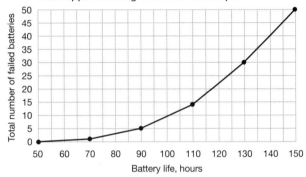

**20.2)** Average value = ((1 × 60) + (4 × 80) + (9 × 100) + (16 × 120) + (20 × 140))/50 [1] = 120 hours [1]

**20.3)** 50% of the batteries = 25 batteries [1] Reading from the graph, this equates to a battery life of 124 hours [1].

**20.4)** The relationship is exponential [1], so the halfway point on the graph (50% of components) is lower than the average [1].

**21. 21.1)** 1 mark for each advantage up to a maximum of 2 marks and 1 mark for an explanation of each up to a maximum of 2 marks. For example, the finished product is more likely to meet user expectations [1] because their needs are considered at all stages [1]. Users have more ownership of the final product [1] meaning they will be more likely to buy it [1].

**21.2)** 1 mark for each disadvantage up to a maximum of 2 marks. For example, takes longer to design the products [1]. Increased expense of implementing suggested changes [1]. Can result in products that are only suited to certain users [1].

**21.3)** 1 mark for each suitable point up to a maximum of 2 marks, such as: an approach used to present a top-down overview of systems [1] by splitting them into input, process and output blocks [1], uses block/systems diagrams to communicate ideas [1]

**22. 22.1)** 1 mark for correct working and 1 mark for correct answer: A = 155 / (tan 30°) [1] A = 268.5 mm [1]

**22.2)** 1 mark for each suitable point up to a maximum of 2 marks: to provide a reference point/surface [1] from which measurements can then be taken [1].

**22.3)** 1 mark for each valid method up to a maximum of 2 marks, such as: nesting [1], use of jigs/patterns/templates [1].

**23. 23.1)** 1 mark for each valid response up to a maximum of 2 marks. For example, papers and boards – printing [1], embossing [1], UV varnishing [1]; Timbers – painting [1], varnishing [1], tanalising [1], painting [1], waxing [1]; Metals – dip-coating [1], powder coating [1], galvanising [1], painting [1]; Polymers – polishing [1], printing [1], application of vinyl decals [1]; Textiles – printing [1], applying dyes and stain protection [1]; Systems – PCB lacquering [1], lubrication [1]

**23.2)** 1 mark for each valid reason up to a maximum of 2 marks, such as: for visual/aesthetic reasons **[1]**, to protect against corrosion/oxidation/wear/damage, etc. **[1]**

**23.3)** 1 mark for each point describing or showing the application of the surface treatment or finish, up to a maximum of 5 marks. For example, varnishing timber – sand wood to create a smooth surface **[1]**, apply filler to any holes **[1]**, use a brush to apply wood sealer or primer **[1]**, apply the varnish **[1]**, add additional coats as necessary **[1]**, allow sufficient time for each coat to dry **[1]**. Galvanising steel – clean the steel **[1]**, place in a molten zinc bath **[1]** of around 460° **[1]**, hold until the steel reaches the desired temperature **[1]** and the bond between the steel and zinc is formed **[1]**, quench the steel **[1]**. Applying vinyl decals to polymer – use a craft knife/vinyl cutter to cut the decals **[1]** from the vinyl sheet **[1]**, peel off the decals from the paper backing **[1]**, position accurately on the plastic surface **[1]**, ensure pressed smoothly onto the plastic surface **[1]**.

**24.1)** 1 mark for each suitable point up to a maximum of 2 marks: when a designer is not able to move past the first design idea/does not explore the full range of design options **[1]**, leading to potentially good design solutions being missed **[1]**.

**24.2)** 1 mark for each suitable point up to a maximum of 3 marks, such as: to test how the product/system would work **[1]**; to show to users/clients **[1]** so they can suggest improvements **[1]**; to see how the product would look in 3D **[1]**; to spot errors in the design **[1]** so they can be corrected before manufacturing of the final product/system begins **[1]**.

# Notes

# Revision Tips

## Rethink Revision

Have you ever taken part in a quiz and thought '*I know this*!', but, despite frantically racking your brain, you just couldn't come up with the answer?

It's very frustrating when this happens, but in a fun situation it doesn't really matter. However, in your GCSE exams, it will be essential that you can recall the relevant information quickly when you need to.

Most students think that revision is about making sure you **know** stuff. Of course, this is important, but it is also about becoming confident that you can **retain** that *stuff* over time and **recall** it quickly when needed.

## Revision That Really Works

Experts have discovered that there are two techniques that help with all of these things and consistently produce better results in exams compared to other revision techniques.

Applying these techniques to your GCSE revision will ensure you get better results in your exams and will have all the relevant knowledge at your fingertips when you start studying for further qualifications, like AS and A Levels, or begin work.

It really isn't rocket science either – you simply need to:

- **test yourself** on each topic as many times as possible
- **leave a gap** between the test sessions.

It is most effective if you leave a good period of time between the test sessions, e.g. between a week and a month. The idea is that just as you start to forget the information, you force yourself to recall it again, keeping it fresh in your mind.

## Three Essential Revision Tips

1. **Use Your Time Wisely**
   - Allow yourself plenty of time.
   - Try to start revising six months before your exams – it's more effective and less stressful.
   - Your revision time is precious so use it wisely – using the techniques described on this page will ensure you revise effectively and efficiently and get the best results.
   - Don't waste time re-reading the same information over and over again – it's time-consuming and not effective!

2. **Make a Plan**
   - Identify all the topics you need to revise (this Complete Revision & Practice book will help you).
   - Plan at least five sessions for each topic.
   - One hour should be ample time to test yourself on the key ideas for a topic.
   - Spread out the practice sessions for each topic – the optimum time to leave between each session is about one month but, if this isn't possible, just make the gaps as big as realistically possible.

3. **Test Yourself**
   - Methods for testing yourself include: quizzes, practice questions, flashcards, past papers, explaining a topic to someone else, etc.
   - This Complete Revision & Practice book provides seven practice opportunities per topic.
   - Don't worry if you get an answer wrong – provided you check what the correct answer is, you are more likely to get the same or similar questions right in future!

Visit our website to download your free flashcards, for more information about the benefits of these revision techniques, and for further guidance on how to plan ahead and make them work for you.

## www.collins.co.uk/collinsGCSErevision

## ACKNOWLEDGEMENTS

The author and publisher are grateful to the copyright holders for permission to use quoted materials and images.

p.14 © David Gee 1 / Alamy Stock Photo
p.93 © www.optitex.com
All other images © Shutterstock.com

Every effort has been made to trace copyright holders and obtain their permission for the use of copyright material. The author and publisher will gladly receive information enabling them to rectify any error or omission in subsequent editions. All facts are correct at time of going to press.

Published by Collins
An imprint of HarperCollins*Publishers* Ltd
1 London Bridge Street
London SE1 9GF

HarperCollins*Publishers*
Macken House, 39/40 Mayor Street Upper,
Dublin 1, D01 C9W8, Ireland

© HarperCollins*Publishers* Limited 2022

ISBN 9780008535018

First published 2017
This edition published 2022

10 9 8 7 6 5 4 3 2

British Library Cataloguing in Publication Data.

A CIP record of this book is available from the British Library.

Authored by: Paul Anderson and David Hills-Taylor
Project management and editorial: Nik Prowse and Shelley Teasdale
Commissioning: Katherine Wilkinson, Clare Souza and Katie Galloway
Cover Design: Kevin Robbins and Sarah Duxbury
Inside Concept Design: Sarah Duxbury and Paul Oates
Text Design and Layout: Jouve India Private Limited
Production: Molly McNevin
Printed in India by Multivista Global Pvt. Ltd

This book contains FSC™ certified paper and other controlled sources to ensure responsible forest management.

For more information visit: www.harpercollins.co.uk/green